Praise for *The Saints Among Us*

"No one in America has given us more valuable insights into our culture and church than George Gallup. This book, co-authored with Timothy Jones, provides a unique combination of statistical analysis for which Gallup is foremost known, human interest stories and cultural critique. It is not only good and informative reading, it is inspiring."

Charles W. Colson
Chairman, Prison Fellowship
Noted author and speaker

"Words such as 'holiness' and 'sainthood' do not come easily to most Americans. When it comes to spiritual and moral heroism, we are embarrassed, tongue-tied, and maybe intimidated by secular pressures. *The Saints Among Us* is an invitation to acknowledge and rejoice in the obvious. God is still making saints and, if we stop fighting it, we may find ourselves among them. This book should carry the warning that it may be dangerous to the reader's contentment with being anything less than a saint."

Richard John Neuhaus
President, The Institute on Religion and Public Life
Editor in Chief, First Things

"George Gallup has become one of the most level-headed religious probers and thinkers among us. With all the data he juggles, I don't see how he keeps such a clear perspective on it all. In his deepening search of that terrain, he has unearthed a new species of believer, personified in his new book—healthier, happier, and with a fuller life than most of us. They make one envious."

George W. Cornell, Religion Writer
Associated Press

"Do you want to grow toward sainthood? You need inspiring role models, people who live a life 'open to a transcendent God.' My first suggestion is that you read this book. It may be life-changing."

Mike McManus
Syndicated Columnist

The Saints Among Us

George H. Gallup, Jr.
Timothy Jones

MOREHOUSE PUBLISHING
Harrisburg, PA

Morehouse Publishing
P.O. Box 1321
Harrisburg, PA 17105

Library of Congress Cataloging-in-Publication Data
Gallup, George, 1930-
The saints among us / George H. Gallup, Jr., Timothy Jones.
p. cm.
Includes bibliographical references.
ISBN 0-8192-1589-9 (pbk.)
1. Christian saints—United States—Public opinion. 2. United States—Public opinion. I. Jones, Timothy 1955- II. Title.
BX4659.U6G35 1992
270'.092'2—dc20 92-12681
[B] CIP

Printed in the United States of America
by
BSC LITHO
Harrisburg, PA 17105

Second Printing, 1993

Dedication

To George O'Connell,

who was inspired by the saints among us

until the very end.

Acknowledgments

The authors express appreciation to

William Beasley, Myrna Grant, Karen Mains,

Kevin Miller, and Jill Zook-Jones

for

carefully reading

significant portions of the manuscript.

Their suggestions helped the stories

of the saints among us come alive.

Contents

Introduction

This book grew out of a quest—an intensive search. We set out to find Americans for whom God is a vibrant reality. We went looking for people who demonstrate that Christian commitment makes a difference in how they actually live. Along the way, we discovered that many—pastors, church members, and secular seekers—shared our fascination. Our question was theirs: Where can we find people with a living, life-changing faith?

A friend who learned of our research told us something intriguing about her own search. She and her family sometimes ask dinner guests and new acquaintances, "Who are your heroes?"

Often, she said, they respond, "Well, I guess I don't have any."

Many Americans would give a similar answer. For all their looking, they have few shining lights. In *The Day America Told the Truth*, researchers James Patterson and Peter Kim say that 70 percent of us believe that America has no living heroes. About the same number say our children have no meaningful role models. Patterson and Kim also note, "The overwhelming majority of people (93 percent) said that they—and nobody else—determine what is and what isn't moral in their lives. They base their decisions on their own experience, even on their daily whims."[1] Indeed, Boston University president John Silber argues in *Straight Shooting* that society sometimes ridicules the mere thought of an admirable person.[2] We are "shy of heroes," someone once said, and we recoil at the idea of admitting that someone is generous or wise or spiritually committed. The ones our culture exalts—the superstars of stage and gridiron—are, in fact, *celebrities.* We are usually drawn to their entertaining qualities, not their personal character or profound maturity.

Sometimes, however, people do come up with an answer to our friend's question. And usually the heroes they mention are surprisingly undistinguished. "I had a great aunt . . ." they will begin, or a parent, a schoolteacher, or a neighbor. And they will proceed to describe someone—a "hero"—who made a deep impression simply through his or her everyday integrity or authentic religious faith. Often the person showed some special quality of caring.

Aren't these the kind of people we would like to know more about—and sit down with, and learn from?

In a real sense, this book allows us to dc just that. We have used the simple tools of survey research to find America's everyday saints. In the aftermath of what some have called the Me Decade, in a day when scandals involving business, political, and even religious leaders have disappointed us, this book can provide new models for how to believe and behave. For a culture searching for basic goodness, these saints can be icons of virtue and maturity. Their lives are like the proverbial picture—worth a thousand words.

How did we find these "saints among us"—those Americans who actually live out their convictions and ideals? How did we learn what they are like?

First, the Gallup Organization, which has been polling Americans about their beliefs and behavior for almost six decades, developed a simple set of twelve questions to lead us to these quietly heroic and faithful individuals. Appendix A shows the twelve questions we asked 1,052 Americans. (We also used the questionnaire in a "purposive sample" approach to lead us to additional saints for our in-depth interviews.) The questions in the surveys focused on such things as the practice of prayer, beliefs about Christ, and the importance ascribed to religious faith. The saints among us are those who answered that they "strongly agreed" or "agreed" to all twelve questions. They made up 13 percent of our sample.

To compare their *behavior* with that of the American public at large, we asked six questions about such things as willingness to help those in need, attitudes toward people of other races, and ability to forgive when wronged. The saints, we found, live noticeably different, more authentic Christian lives.

However intriguing those results are (as we will see later), this book is far more than a compendium of figures. We also interviewed—by mail, phone, and personal visits—a wide range of saints among us, from all walks of life, all age groups, a full gamut of denominations, and every region of the country. We thereby discovered the vibrancy and staying power of a substantial number of Americans' faith. Their stories—many dramatic, others more subtly inspiring—will appear throughout this book. We will introduce readers to a young black Baptist woman from the South who overcame crushing prejudice and personal bitterness, an Episcopal office manager who is quietly introducing colleagues to faith, a Catholic woman from coastal New England who talks to God in ways that change her life, and others. We believe that the reader will experience, as we did, a sense of serendipity akin to that of a medical researcher making a breakthrough in a laboratory setting. The stories of the saints make it difficult to resist the conclusion that God is indeed at work in the lives of people today.

Of course, trying to put "calipers" on spiritual experience and practice has limitations. Faith cannot be reduced to charts and tables. It cannot be dissected with the tools of the laboratory scientist. Also, because our polls relied largely on self-assessment, those with higher self-esteem likely scored higher than those with low self-esteem when asked about their faith (although our follow-up interviews by phone and in person helped verify our data).

And while the Gallup Organization worked closely with religious leaders, sociologists, and other experts in formulating the survey apparatus, not everyone will agree how religious commitment is best defined or most accurately measured. Not every person would agree with our choice of survey questions, or with their generally Christian orientation. We also recognize the seeming presumption in trying to quantify the personal and sometimes numinous character of religious experience. Indeed, only God knows the intentions and motivations of the heart. Finally, our sample size made it difficult to draw conclusions about Jewish and Muslim believers, since their percentages in our population are relatively small. Given the number surveyed, our numbers would be statistically insignificant. We have, then, limited our conclusions to Christian saints, and have chosen to orient the book within the framework of Christian faith and practice.

However imperfect any such survey must be, our survey allowed us to conclude once for all that around us and among us are people who truly live what they profess. They may not be canonized or officially recognized, but they find deep meaning in prayer. They gain personal strength from their religious convictions. And they demonstrate more than mere religious sentiment. They often spend significant time helping people burdened with physical and emotional needs. They are less likely to be prejudiced against people of other races, and are more giving, and more forgiving. They have bucked the trend of many in society toward narcissism and privatism.

We have found that these "hidden saints" (to use a phrase of Pope John Paul II) are the backbone of our communities and churches. They are like the yeast Jesus described in one of his parables: their presence is quiet, subtle—but unmistakable. They seem to live out the twin commands Jesus said were essential to genuine religion: to love God with heart and soul and mind, and to love neighbor as self (Matt. 22:37-39). From this 13 percent, we can extrapolate and suggest that they are 24 million strong out of an adult U.S. population of 182 million. They can be found in virtually every neighborhood, public school, office building, and congregation.

For a society tempted to think that only a highly visible few—the Billy Grahams and Mother Teresas—make a difference, our research shows otherwise. Our interviews with the friends, associates, and neighbors of the saints among us lead us to conclude that they have an impact on society far out of proportion to their numbers. In the chapters that follow, we talk about how the saints have found a living spirituality in our secular times and learned the lessons of compassion. We explain why we have concluded that saints lead noticeably happier, more fulfilled lives. We detail the intriguing finding that the saints among us are more likely to be nonwhite, female, and Southern. They are, in other words, the very ones that society often looks *last* to for help or role models. Finally, we suggest how churches, organizations, and families can learn from the saints among us—and help others become like them.

"It is not so much a question of where to look to find saints," John Delaney writes, "rather it is merely the need to remove the blinders from our eyes, for saints are here in our age just as they have been in every age for the past two millennia."[3] The research documented in this book confirms that our age is indeed no different. As we meet the everyday heroes described in this book, they can lead us to discover a deeper faith and truer commitment in the nineties and beyond.

1

A Picture Worth a Thousand Words

Many of us have, often subconsciously, accepted the premise that saints are of the past.
—John Delaney[1]

Only God makes saints. Still, it is up to us to tell their stories.
—Kenneth Woodward[2]

On a tree-lined, almost rustic road an hour's drive from metropolitan Chicago, Dotty Biros lives with her husband and four children in an unremarkable brick ranch house. Their home, set back from the road and partly hidden by towering oaks and spruces, would be easy to miss. Not surprisingly, the middle-aged housewife is barely known beyond her circle of neighbors and friends. In some ways she lives a simple, unspectacular life. But only in *some* ways.

She is one of a special group of Americans, some of whom we will meet in this book, whose lives have a kind of quiet drama. These are everyday people who make an extraordinary difference, people we call saints among us.

"When our two-and-a-half-year-old son died," one of Dotty's friends remembers, "Dotty was the one person who got me through it. She could tell by looking at you when you needed to talk. I couldn't have gotten through without her."

Sarah Blalock, another friend, remembers going into a dangerous premature labor with her second child, while her husband, to top it off, was hospitalized. "Dotty took me and my daughter in to live with her until my mother could arrive from out of town to help. Even friends I knew longer or was closer to didn't offer to help like that."

Mere helpfulness, however, does not explain all that is different about Dotty. Friends describe an indefinable radiance. "Her eyes glow when she speaks of her faith," one observes. "When it comes to her religious commitment, you can just see it in her. Even if her hair's not fixed, her makeup not put on, you look at her eyes, and she's beautiful."

For all the good she does, almost no one beyond her immediate circle of friends, family, and neighbors has even heard her name. Even at the nearby Episcopal church, where she helps lead a small Bible study and sharing group, teaches Sunday school, and takes food to members in need, Dotty is not one of the first persons a visitor will meet on a Sunday morning. She is no celebrity.

And as she tells her own story, you soon sense that she also has no illusions about being perfect. She admits that life has been a struggle at times, including the pain of a failed first marriage, a deeply disappointing miscarriage, and periods of religious doubt and uncertainty.

Indeed, her first steps toward faith were seemingly accidental. As a child of ten, born into a non-churchgoing family, she ended up at church because it was the "thing to do for girls my age." She made her first commitment a couple of years later, not out of any great conviction, but because a friend had told her, "My mom says I can't play with you anymore if you don't go forward for an altar call" (a fixture of the worship of the revival-style church she attended).

During teen years she gave up church, finding her way back as an adult. Even then, she remembers, "I went to church just because it felt good, and because when I didn't, I could tell a difference in my week. But when it came to worship itself, I had trouble keeping my mind on what was being said or what was going on. I would think about things I had to do during the week." Something, however changed that: Dotty miscarried, and, she recalls, she "went crazy with grief." It was then that Dotty's nurse, perhaps herself a saint among us, intervened. The nurse was a Christian, Dotty remembers, and gave of herself in a remarkable way: "Even though she had a family, she would come and spend time with me at my home on my day off. I remember that it was the first time I felt that there was a real difference in someone who claimed to know the Lord. Through our talks I realized my need for God, that I could not get through the death of a child without him."

As we will see, this was only one step on Dotty's journey toward faith. We will also see how she is just one of what we estimate to be 24 million Americans. In the cynicism and disillusionment of our day, she and her colleagues in informal sainthood are people worth noting.

Of course, the proportion of Americans who claim faith far exceeds 13 percent. Ninety-four percent of Americans say they believe in "God or some kind of unseen spirit." Eighty-four percent view God as the "heavenly father of the Bible who can be reached by prayers." And 43 percent claimed they attended church in a typical week in 1989.[3] For all that, however, we have not really known the details about how faith actually makes a difference in the lives of those—like Dotty—who seem to take it very seriously. Polling over the years has helped us gauge the breadth, but it has not usually helped us see the depth.

WHERE WE FOUND THE SAINTS

Figures below represent percentages of saints among us.

Region	**Percent**
East	5
Midwest	13
South	22
West	10
(National	13)

Occupation	**Percent**
Professional and business	9
Other white collar	7
Blue collar	12

Mere church membership, for example, does not necessarily indicate authentic, transforming faith. Years of polls show scant difference between the churched and unchurched in terms of cheating, tax evasion, and pilferage. Disturbingly, *Psychology Today* reported an experiment in which researchers found that seminary students on their way to an appointment "often walked right past a man slumped over and groaning in a doorway. Some of the subjects were on their way to give a talk on the parable of the Good Samaritan. If they were late, they were no more likely to stop and help than others."[4]

In other words, faith seems to be a largely private affair for many. In *Habits of the Heart*, sociologist Robert Bellah and his colleagues gave the intriguing profile of a young nurse, Sheila Larson, whose faith she describes as "Sheilaism." She says it's "just my own little voice." She believes in God, after a fashion, but in defining "my own Sheilaism," she says, it's "just try and love yourself and be gentle with yourself. You know, I guess, take care of each other."[5]

There appears to be a great deal of self-centered, provincial faith—extrinsic religion, as psychologist Gordon Allport called it—that makes little difference in people's lives. Extrinsic faith tends to be more institution-centered, and primarily something to be called on in crisis. The prevalence of this type of faith perhaps explains why in repeated surveys only one American in four says that religion is the "most important" influence in his or her life.

Why saint sounds like a bad word

However we might admire the highly committed, the word "saint" sometimes elicits images of naive do-gooders. Saintliness may seem out of step with a world where ozone holes, ICBM missiles, and "crack" babies call for hard-hitting pragmatism. And "it is probable," said a wry George Bernard Shaw, "that some who achieve or aspire to sainthood have never felt much the temptation to be human beings."

But the saints identified by our research evidence little pie-in-the-sky escapism. They seem planted firmly in the gritty substance of everyday life. True, many list an otherworldly reality—the assurance of eternal life in heaven—as one reward of faith. But our research also suggests that the greater the place religion is given in respondents' lives (as reflected in the twelve-item spiritual commitment scale described in the introduction and Appendix A), the more dramatic the impact on everyday behavior. The saints have a disproportionately powerful impact upon society's day-to-day functioning in terms of the sum total of charitable acts and quiet volunteerism. They are responsible for our society being kinder, more tolerant, forgiving, and optimistic. They are the salt and light of our world.

How do we know? We also asked respondents to answer six questions (in addition to the twelve on spiritual commitment) about their willingness to help others, their attitudes toward persons of other races, and their openness to forgiving others when wronged. Fascinating differences emerged. The group that scored highest on the spiritual commitment scale also scored highest on this statement: "I spend a good deal of time helping people in physical, emotional, or other kinds of needs." Seventy-three percent of the saints among us (those who answered "strongly agree" or "agree" to the twelve statements) said they are active in helping others. These saints, we found, are not so "heavenly minded" that they are of no earthly good.

In addition, our research indicates that the absence of spiritual commitment makes people less likely to show compassion. Among respondents answering "disagree" or "strongly disagree" to all twelve spiritual commitment statements, only 42 percent said they help those in need. The greater the "spiritual commitment," in other words, the greater the expressed concern for others; the less the spiritual commitment, the less involvement in helping others. Compassion, tolerance, and ethical behavior consistently rise as spiritual commitment increases.

HOW GROUPS SHAPE THE SAINTS

Figures below represent percentages of saints among us.

Within denominations	Percent
Catholic	11
Protestant	17

Within political parties*	Percent
Republican	13
Democrat	15
Independent	11

**Little statistical difference found.*

G.K. Chesterton, English journalist of decades ago, once said that if he were a landlord, what he would most want to know about his tenants was not their employment or their income, but their beliefs. One of the most dramatic of our findings concerns the substantial connection between beliefs and behavior.

We found that the saints, when describing their struggle to be more loving, indeed repeatedly mentioned a religious teaching or instance of God's "leading." Their motivations were often spiritual. One saint among us, for example, described her motivation for working with people with disabilities in this way: "Christ treated everybody, whether disabled or poor, with dignity and respect. That's what I try to do." Another spoke of faith helping her "look beyond the person to the soul that God loves so much. Therefore how much more compassion can I have!" Others were not so articulate. It was as though concern for others became so deeply ingrained that, as one saint said, it becomes "second nature."

We also came to suspect that sometimes spiritual beliefs were the final ounce that tipped the saints' inner scales on the side of overcoming hestitation and actually reaching out to another. When we asked a retired nurse living in Nashville how she recently went out of her way to do or say something because she "believed it was in accordance with God's will," she told us, "Someone very close to me hurt me. I took the lead in accepting a difficult situation and initiated reconciliation. This wasn't easy because I'm somewhat shy and reserved by nature." One saint from Natick, Massachusetts, a quiet Boston suburb where once lived the nineteenth-century abolitionists Henry Ward Beecher and Harriet Beecher Stowe, tells this story: "While driving on a small local road, I noticed a young woman hitchhiking. Although I never stop for hitchhikers, I felt God wanted me to pick her up. As we drove together, I talked extensively to her about recovery and emotional healing. She was on heroin and her life was pretty messed up. I talked with her about Christ, and helped her pray a prayer of acceptance of Christ and of help from God. Though I have never heard from her, I know God led me to give her a ride so he could give her a message of hope." It seems the saints, as one of the friends of the authors put it, "actually *do*—they *act* in ways the rest of us just talk about." Better than most, we found, the saints among us close the gap between intention and concrete action, between aspiration and deed.

We confirmed that the saints are different, and are making a difference, because in some instances we approached their neighbors and colleagues. Ray Pool from Canoga Park, California, is a good example. He takes his evangelical faith very seriously, combining active church involvement with praying daily with his wife for global leaders and next-door neighbors. When we tracked down one of his neighbors, who does not share Ray's religious commitment, we learned that his spiritual life is more than pious sentiment. She spoke of the way the Pools are always ready with offers of child care, or sometimes just a listening ear. She noted, "Almost always, when I realize people are strongly religious, like Ray, I discover they are also supportive and generous."

When imitation is not second best

It is one thing to be encouraged by instances of faith truly "working." But beyond that, why care?

We believe that the saints among us are more than encouraging spiritual success stories. We present sketches of their lives and their experiences here because we believe that they can provide new models, new heroes for an age in search of moral and spiritual leadership. Without them, the church—to say nothing of society—would be crippled in forming the faith and character of its members. Developmental theorists have long argued that modeling—not just teaching or speaking—is a cornerstone of human growth toward maturity.

Indeed, "without examples, without imitation," historian Robert Wilken writes, "there can be no human life or civilization, no art or culture, no virtue or holiness. The elementary activities of . . . learning to speak or sculpting a statue, have their beginning in the imitation of what others do." Wilken draws a conclusion about how we can benefit from the saints among us: "By observing the lives of holy men and women and imitating their deeds we become virtuous. Before we can become doers we must first become spectators."[6]

Wilken also observes that stories of saintly and heroic believers do not so much "present us with a new theory of virtue, but a new way of teaching, a new strategy that builds on the tradition of examples, but enriches it by unfolding a pattern of holiness over the course of a lifetime. Precepts are now put in the mouths of familiar persons, and examples are enhanced by seeing them as deeds of specific individuals."[7]

Other eras have known this. This is why holy heroes are so important in the Old Testament. From the earliest days of Christianity, when Paul the apostle wrote to the church at Philippi, "Take note of those who live according to the pattern we gave you" (Phil. 3:17, NIV), believers have known that having models to emulate is essential to spiritual growth. Interestingly, Christians from about the fourth century A.D. onward wrote and cherished biographies of the faithful known as "Lives of the Saints." These "lives" emphasize seeing and watching another holy life to gain understanding in how to live one's own. This interest, of course, flowered in later centuries of Roman Catholicism and Eastern Orthodoxy. Indeed, Catholics and some Orthodox pray to saints and treasure their relics. They believe saints can effect miracles from their exalted place in heaven. Their canonized saints now number in the hundreds.

While Protestants reject the Catholic notion that saints are mediators in our relationship with God, they, too, know that we need heroes and mentors, from Augustine to Martin Luther to Martin Luther King, Jr. We need people who have applied the call to faith and sanctity to their own times and challenges. And we need the stories of the everyday saints, not just church history's "celebrities."

A modest cloud of witnesses

If there is value in imitation, there is also limitation. The saints we profile are real people. They would be the first to admit that their lives are unfinished and imperfect. "I'm no saint," more than one of them warned when we approached them for conversation. Our interviews suggest that they are not smug and unrealistic about themselves, that faith is a growth process they will never, at least in this life, complete. They do not always give themselves a perfect score on tolerance, or loving others. They are as likely to say they cheat on their taxes as the general population. (Five percent say they sometimes "claim too many deductions" or "don't report" all income on their tax returns, whereas the percentage for the general population is six.) One saint among us admitted that his life is not always a shining example, especially, as he put it, "when I get around my friends, the guys I grew up with, who haven't accepted Christ. Sometimes it's too easy to just play it neutral and sit on the fence. I'd love to be able to tell you that I have people come up to me all the time and tell me what a changed life I'm living. I don't. But I have the faith that there will be growth, that God will keep working with me."

One saint, a young mother and schoolteacher, admitted, "There have been some crisis times when I felt like I couldn't find God." Indeed, last year she suffered serious depression. "I was under a lot of pressures. Our church's pastor had died of cancer. Our choir director committed suicide the month before that. The pressures of coping put a lot of stress on my marriage." She felt things were hitting her from "every direction, and a lot of times when I prayed, I felt like it was just bouncing back at me." Only emotional support from relatives and the insight of a counselor helped her regain normalcy. But seemingly ordinary people, we will see, can do extraordinary things, and inspire and instruct us. God rides the lame horse and carves the rotten wood, Martin Luther once said—by which he meant that God uses imperfect people.

Besides, as Kenneth Woodward, quoting John Coleman, notes, "The attraction of saints . . . 'is their power to lure us beyond virtue to virtue's source.'"[8] What is truly encouraging about them is not just their commitment and compassion, but the suggestion that we, too, can live with a new awareness of God, that we can aspire to something more in our relations with others. Their lives should be not an occasion for measuring how far we fall short, but a living word of encouragement for what life can be. Like the real-life saints portrayed in this book, the vast majority of this book's readers will not draw crowds when they speak, will not be able to convince world leaders to make peace, and will lead lives filled with everyday, very often mundane responsibilities. The stories we tell here testify that no one should overlook the significance of an inauspicious moment of quiet prayer, or of the bag of groceries delivered to a food pantry for the needy, without which we would not have society as we know it. If our stories provide role models that can inspire and instruct an age convinced that meaning is found in what we can buy and grasp for ourselves, it will be because they come from the arena of everyday life, from the lives of the simple, even hidden believers among us.

These stories can also help us when we tire of the struggle to be better, reminding us that we are not alone in our effort, that others have done what we are trying so doggedly to accomplish. As the English writer Evelyn Underhill notes, when we observe or spend time with the spiritually committed "we seem to catch something from them and obtain from them a secret and invisible support. In the saints we always have the society of inspiring Christians, are always in touch with the classic standard."[9]

A friend of one of the authors tells of coming back to the church of her childhood after years of being away. One of the first Sundays after she returned, one of the hymns in the service was "I Sing a Song of the Saints of God." "They lived not only in ages past," she sang, "there are hundreds of thousands still, the world is bright with the joyous saints who love to do Jesus' will. You can meet them in school, or in lanes, or at sea, in church, or in trains, or in shops, or at tea, for the saints of God are just folk like me, and I mean to be one too."[10] She remembers thinking, with a sense of great discovery, "I didn't know it could be a goal for me, that I could aspire to be a saint."

The good news in our book is that sainthood is alive and well. What we can learn holds great promise for us and for those we live and work with and serve.

2

The Saints Among Us in Profile

A saint is a living epistle written by the finger of God, known and read of all men.
—Oswald Chambers[1]

Take note of those who live according to the pattern we gave you.
—Paul the Apostle[2]

From the start, our search for the saints among us showed us that they are as different from one another as they are alike. We found that no single group of American Christians can claim a copyright on saintliness—not Protestants or Catholics, nor high achievers or disadvantaged, nor men or women. The saints among us experience life-changing encounters with God irrespective of most social and theological categories. They defy many of our preconceptions and expectations.

When it comes to their ages, for example, they are more likely to be fifty or older (the passing of years does indeed seem to bring spiritual maturity). But they also span a wide range of adult ages, and include "baby busters" and "boomers," a significant finding in light of society's stereotype of these groups as excessively me-centered.

The tapestry of the lives of the saints among us has other variegated threads. Saints are rich and poor alike (though those who earn less than $10,000 a year are more likely to be saints). They are doctors, factory workers, homemakers, and the unemployed. Their vocabulary comes from church traditions as distinct as rural Pentecostal and mainline Protestant. A larger proportion may be found in the South, but their number is scattered across every region of the country. You are more likely to find saints among nonwhite groups, though no single ethnic group has a monopoly. They relate a great variety of personal stories and experiences.

For all the variety, to which we will return later, the saints among us have several things in common. These are the traits that set them apart and make us want to get the feel of their faith.

Margie Dennie is a twenty-nine-year-old black woman from a community of townhouses in a working-class community just ouside Chicago. She is back in college, after a hiatus of several years, to gain her teacher's certification, while her husband serves as an associate pastor at a nearby Baptist church. Like Dotty Biros, she is in many ways typical and representative of the saints among us.

Says a long-time acquaintance, "Margie believes in making the world a better place. She and her husband both have college degrees and could have chosen lucrative careers. But she's planning on being a schoolteacher and her husband is a pastor—not high-paying professions, but ones in which they can serve people." Her friends are struck by her steady contentment, all the more remarkable, as we will see later, in light of some of the hardships of her earlier life. "She wasn't exactly born with a silver spoon in her mouth," notes her friend. We will feature her story prominently throughout this chapter because it will allow us to lift up the common characteristics of the many saints we surveyed.

WHAT DOES A SAINT LOOK LIKE?

Figures below represent percentages of saints among us.

Sex	Percent
Men	11
Women	15

Race	Percent
White	12
Nonwhite	22
Black	24
Hispanic	9

Age	Percent
18-29	10
30-49	10
50 and older	19

Level of Education	Percent
College graduates	10
Incomplete college & technical school	11
High school graduates	14
Less than high school	18

Six Characteristics of the Saints Among Us

The saints' experience of God

First, Margie, like the other saints we talked with, has found God to be a vital part of daily life and personal experience. A friend notes, "When I've heard her pray, I think she 'touches' God. She calls him Father, and it sounds like she really means it." Her keen awareness of spiritual realities can be traced back to a not-so-easy early childhood spent in Clarksville, Mississippi.

"I didn't grow up in a traditional home with a loving father," she remembers. "My parents weren't married, my father was not around, and much of my early childhood I lived with my grandparents. I turned to God a lot of times for the comfort that would otherwise be given by parents. That's when I began to feel God's presence and love in my life. I would talk to him, and would hear a little voice inside telling me I was special. As I got older, I grew away from that dependence on God. I began to form other relationships." Most important in this process was her moving to Chicago at age eight to rejoin her mother. "I didn't depend on the Lord quite so much for comfort. But I still had a little voice inside telling me I'm special. I began to call God my Father."

When it came to her natural father, however, Margie began to experience a longing to meet him, a desire that was to have great spiritual ramifications. She prayed that God would help her find him, and she soon found her father's address. The letter she wrote found its way to him in a remarkable way that she credits as an answer to prayer.

"I didn't know it at the time, but my father no longer lived in the house where I had sent the letter." He had left months before, when his mother, with whom he shared the house, died. The house sat vacant for months. When a relative was preparing the house for selling, Margie relates, "a voice told him to open the mailbox," and there, after months of neglect, lay Margie's letter, which was passed on immediately to her father. He received the letter, and contact was made.

"Not knowing my father had been a big void in my life. Many times I would cry out, 'God, I just want to know my daddy!' . . . When I finally found him, from that point on I said, God, you know what's best for me. You know me in ways nobody else could. You are the only one who could know how important this was to me."

As she tells the story from her home, she speaks quietly, with little dramatic flourish, about her beliefs in God's palpable reality in her life. As we found with the other saints among us, God seems to be not just an article of belief, but a living reality. This is evident on several scores.

On the simplest level, this means the saints among us can all agree to statements like these: "I seek God's will through prayer," "I believe that God loves me even though I may not always obey him," and "I receive comfort and support from my religious beliefs." This is not so remarkable in itself, in that other Gallup research reveals that 88 percent of Americans pray to God. Some 76 percent agree that prayer is "an important part" of their daily lives.[3] There is an enormous amount of personal piety in the U.S.

The saints, however, manifest a measurably different understanding of the role of the Spirit. In our follow-up interviews, they repeatedly made mention of a moment of religious insight or awakening as central to their understanding of life and service. When we asked in our a follow-up mail interview to several dozen, "Have you ever had a religous experience—that is, a particularly powerful religious insight or awakening?" the vast majority of those that responded said yes.

This only confirms what other polls have already shown us: The strongest believers are those who believe that God has intervened in their lives, who are convinced that God can be known and can act.

A different level of commitment

Second, the saints among us not only experience God in a deep way, but they also respond with exceptional commitment. In a day when people hold themselves aloof from strong religious loyalty (the percentage of Americans who "strongly agree" that faith is the most important influence in their lives is 22 percent),[4] the saints cut a different profile.

Margie Dennie exemplies what we mean. At age sixteen, after finally finding her father, she recalls, "I gave my life totally over to God. He had revealed himself to me in such a clear way. He had been there in the midst of all my wishes, hurts, sorrows—and understood. From that point I said, if you can be there in that way for me, Lord, I just want to be your servant, and do what you want me to do."

Her commitment held, even when in high school friends began to "get interested in drugs and parties." Studying the Bible and being around Christians convinced her that her non-Christian friends' lifestyle "was not pleasing to the Lord. I had to make a lot of difficult choices. But commitment to him was more important than any friendship."

This coming to a place of reckoning, of making faith the overriding priority in life, takes place in a variety of ways. Our research explodes the idea that people commit themselves to God in only one pattern. There is no "morphology of conversion," no taxonomy for coming to a resounding choice to follow Christ. When asked how they became deeply religious, some saints we met pointed to decisive "crisis" conversions. Others recalled a nurture at home and church so pervasive, or a spiritual hunger so gnawing and continuous, that commitment came gradually and steadily as they grew older.

One of our saints among us, thirty-five-year-old John Fafinski of Elgin, Illinois, illustrates one pattern. He observes, "I am one of those people who has an exact date when he became a believer. During my senior year of college, I found out my roommate was a Christian. At first I didn't want to room with him for that reason. I thought religion was just following a bunch of rules. But by living with him, I saw something different. Finally one night I talked to him at length and ended up kneeling down and praying a very simple prayer, asking the Lord to come into my life."

Sheila Solomon, a saint from rural Fitzwater, Georgia, tells a different story. "I was raised in a Christian home. I could say I went to church nine months before I was born!" She traces her significant commitment to Christ back to age eight. "[But] as I got older, there were times when I wasn't sure that that commitment was sufficient for an adult. When I was twenty-four I made another commitment, what I feel was an adult commitment." Sheila stresses that she sees herself still growing in faith.

Journey inward, journey outward

The saints among us, we found, are not only exceptional in their spirituality and commitment, they are noteworthy in their compassion. The outcome of their "journey inward" toward spiritual reality is often a "journey outward" into the world of need about them. They share more of themselves with others than do less committed Americans.

For Margie Dennie, this has sent her back to school to gain teacher certification. Recalling the difficulty of her early family life and the pain of some childhood experiences of racism, she now wants to do something to help others, because, as she puts it, "I'm seeing a need to educate Christian children in an environment that's safe and welcoming for them. . . . I want to be open to God's leading and the way he'd use me."

The benefit to society of the saints among us must be enormous. As we noted earlier, 73 percent claim to spend a good deal of time helping people in need, whereas with the strongly uncommitted the percentage drops to 42. Whether it's a woman taking her elderly friend to the dentist, or a man who sends letters to the editor of his local newspaper to share his moral convictions about social issues, the saints among us are doing much to express their faith in tangible ways.

Here is how one saint among us from Hanover, Massachusetts, described what she did: "God's love is [so] abundant and real in my life that it just naturally overflows into my conversations." She also noted that when it comes to certain social issues, "I go out of my way to make a difference . . . I write newspapers and senators." Her help went beyond simple service to an attempt to change society.

Others told of specific people they had helped, many in the last twenty-four hours. One gave baby items to a young Korean woman and mother new to the United States. Others helped victims of cancer, went out of their way to visit and pray with the hospitalized, volunteered heavily in church programs, and gave money to charitable causes. One saint we interviewed described how he had become more compassionate and committed to others over the past three or four years. "I've tried to get more involved at my church, teaching Sunday school, for example. And I joined the Lions Club, because I'm trying to get involved through a civic organization to help people less fortunate than I am."

We were struck, however, that much of the work was done on an individual basis. Other than church involvement, few mentioned working with structured volunteer programs such as soup kitchens or homeless shelters. We suspect that the saints among us tend to respond to need when it crosses their paths; they may not be as active in more organized forms of helping. When they are, much of their work seems to take place through local churches.

It is significant to note here the finding of sociologist Robert Wuthnow, who concludes that church and community play a much larger role in keeping faith from stagnating into individualist pietism than previously thought. "Among individuals who attend church infrequently or who do not attend, how much or how little they feel God's love has no effect on the likelihood of their being involved in charitable acts." Religious inclinations seem not to motivate charitable efforts toward the poor or disadvantaged unless the person is involved in some religious organization.[5]

We will say more about this and the shape of the help that the saints give others. Now we simply note that such outward orientation figures prominently in their lives. This confirms our belief that spiritual commitment not only brings happiness to believers, it also turns them into conduits of good to others.

The Catholic monk and activist Thomas Merton wrote that the great saints of history were not only deeply touched by God, they also had a "miraculous power, a smooth and tireless energy" that helped them change others around them and even "the course of religious and even secular history."[6] Some of the great mystics and spiritual giants of the church through the ages were reformers and indefatigable workers. They established hospitals and orphanages that made the contributions of more "earthly-minded" friends pale. The saints have much to show us about how genuine spirituality leads to service.

Color-blind love

A fourth and especially striking finding about the saints among us concerns their lack of prejudice. Eighty-four percent of the saints among us would not object to a person of another race moving in next door. While that may not be a "perfect score," it beats that of the spiritually uncommitted by more than twenty points.

For Margie Dennie, this has meant a profound movement through scars from early prejudice to an attitude of love and acceptance for people of all skin colors.

She tells of growing up black in the deep South in the wake of segregation. In the late sixties, when she was in third grade, that meant leaving her all-black grammar school to be integrated into a previously all-white school on the far side of town. "I remember having to walk a long distance (no busing was provided) through white neighborhoods. People would come to the gates at the edges of their yards with their dogs and tell the animals, 'Git her!' The dogs would be restrained by the fences, but as an eight-year-old I was terrified. Others would cry out derogatory names. I would run and a lot of mornings would cry." Once, while she was waiting for her ride home after school, a car full of white teenagers pulled up and called her nigger and shouted, "You've got soul in the bottom of your shoes."

Six Questions on Commitment

How did the saints fare?

QUESTION	PERCENTAGES*				
	General Population	A	B	C	D
I would not object to a person of a different race moving next door.	80	63	80	84	93
I am very happy.	87	86	86	93	92
I sometimes claim too many deductions or don't report all my income on my tax return.	6	5	6	5	7
I spend a good deal of time helping people in physical, emotional, or other kinds of needs.	66	42	65	73	85
I believe it is important to forgive people who have hurt me deeply.	88	71	87	98	100
I try to follow a strict moral code.	87	71	85	100	100

Column A: Spiritually uncommitted (answered all twelve spiritual commitment questions with disagree or strongly disagree).

Column B: Nonsaints (did not answer all twelve spiritual commitment questions with agree or strongly agree).

Column C: Saints among us (answered all twelve spiritual commitment questions with agree or strongly agree).

Column D: "Supersaints" (answered all twelve spiritual commitment questions with strongly agree).

*Based on a nationally representative sample of 1,052 Americans, surveyed in 1988.

She soon moved to Chicago to escape the tension and rejoin her mother. While attending high school there, the racial issue came to head: "I was the only black on my school bus. It brought back all the old memories. I don't know if it was hatred, or hurt, but I would actually get sick on the bus." She began to pray in desperation, "Lord, I don't want to feel like this. I don't want to hate."

"I don't remember the specifics," she relates, "but I remember one day riding the bus and realizing that I wasn't getting sick anymore. And I knew God was helping me not to hate. He also gave me a friend who was Japanese. I began to see the different cultures, and to realize that not all people were responsible for what happened to me as a child.

"Then, in college, my roommate turned out to be a white woman who was also a Christian. God revealed to me how love can overcome all the differences. As I studied the Bible, I realized anew how, as Paul says, 'there is neither Jew nor Greek' (Gal. 3:28)." Says a friend, "You'd expect a person who's been through what she's been through to be bitter, but she's not."

We can all think of notable exceptions to such a picture, of course, of instances where zealous religiosity is linked to bigotry; of certain segments of fundamentalism that use scripture to justify segregation; of people who have not yet realized the implications of their following Jesus, a friend of tax collectors and social outcasts, whatever the race. And it must be admitted that religious faith at times has seemed to fuel prejudice and intolerance.

Yet it is striking how deep faith can change people's attitudes. This is precisely what we found with many of our saints. When asked about their unprejudiced attitudes, they frequently spoke of God's fatherhood, of the Bible's emphasis on love for neighbor, of how faith lifted them above narrowness to see the presence of God in others.

The happiness factor

Fifth, we found that the saints among us lead more fulfilled lives. They consistently characterized themselves as "very happy": 93 percent of our saints said they were, compared to 86 percent of rest of the population. This was borne out in a similar line of questioning in 1981: 68 percent of the "highly spiritually committed" (those who responded "strongly agree" to seven statements about faith and spiritual life) answered affirmatively to the statement "I am very happy," while only 44 percent of the general population did so.[7]

This happiness is apparently not a superficial experience, but rather an abiding joy. In Margie Dennie's case, as with many of the saints among us, its solidity was tested by difficulty. For all Margie's painful experiences, she spoke of God's intimate care sustaining her. During the peer-pressure temptations of high school, she remembers concluding, "God gave me a keeping power during that time. He gives you confidence for self, love for self, where you wouldn't want to harm your body with drugs or premarital sex." One saint with multiple sclerosis said simply, "If I didn't have God, I'd be down in the dumps, not able to smile or laugh."

Another saint describes the joy that met her upon her baptism as an adult. "I felt forgiven. Suddenly the sky looked brighter, the clouds whiter." When asked to describe the "rewards" of spiritual commitment, respondent after respondent mentioned words like peace, assurance, and joy.

This is all the more striking given the stereotypical belief that religion dampens joy, or that religious faith is stifling and oppressive. "Joy is the echo of God's life within us," writer Joseph Marmion once said. The saints would testify to that.

The last who are first

Finally, the saints among us are often found in surprising places. They give the lie to the assumption that only the well-placed and powerful can make a difference. For example, women, like Margie Dennie yield a disproportionate percentage of saints among us (15 percent of women are saints, as opposed to 11 percent of men). Blacks are twice as likely as whites to be saints among us. Saints are slightly more likely to be found in the South or earn under $25,000 each year. The saints are almost twice as likely to be found among those who did not graduate from high school as among those with college degrees. For the most part, the faith of the saints reveals a simple goodness. They remind us of Jesus' words that in the transformed values of the kingdom the ones that the present world considers the last shall be first. Many come from what society considers the least recognized and least powerful group: the nonwhite, female poor. When we think about the ones who change the course of history, we tend to include the powerful and wealthy, the presidents and their staffs. We think of those with position and education, with leverage and economic advantage. But the saints among us may matter far more. They are making a contribution to society too little recognized, too quickly overlooked.

It is true that the saints we found do not often stride down our government's corridors of power, but their influence, because of its dailyness, is consistent. Many lack formal theological training, but have fashioned a workable faith that works in the push and pull of the businesses, factories, and neighorhoods they inhabit. They also stand close enough to daily need to be humble, not proud. If they stopped to think about it, they could resonate with the apostle Paul's admonishment in 1 Corinthians: "Think of what you were when you were called. Not many of you were wise by human standards; not many were influential; not many were of noble birth. But God chose the foolish things of the world to shame the wise. . . . He chose the lowly things of this world . . . so that no one may boast before him" (1 Cor. 1:26–29 NIV). For all their simplicity, the saints among us leave a mark in our communities and in our lives.

Christian apologist C. S. Lewis wrote of what he called the "new men," the people transformed by faith, who are much like our saints among us. "Already the 'new men' are dotted here and there all over the earth," Lewis wrote. "Every now and then one meets them. Their voices and faces are different from ours, stronger, quieter, happier, more radiant. They begin where most of us leave off. . . . They are . . . recognisable; but you must know what to look for. They will not be very like the idea of 'religious people' which you have formed from your general reading. They do not draw attention to themselves. You tend to think that you are being kind to them when they are really being kind to you. They love you more than other men do, but need you less. . . . When you have recognised one of them, you will recognise the next one much more easily."[9]

3

The Secret of Their Staying Power

Can one be a saint if God does not exist?
That is the only concrete problem I know of today.
—Albert Camus[1]

Grace is indeed needed to turn a man into a saint,
and he who doubts it does not know what a saint or a man is.
—Blaise Pascal[2]

In 1976, when Allen Danforth was a thirty-six-year-old Houston banker, something happened that would change his life forever. "I had been searching for God on my own terms," the rugged looking fifty-two-year-old resident of Little Rock, Arkansas, remembers. "I was involved with the occult. I thought of God as magnetism, or some Star Wars 'force.' He was everywhere, but a 'nonpersonality.'"

While he doesn't dwell on the details in the telling, Allen talks about having a "confrontation with the demonic." That's when the change began. "I became aware, first of all, that what I was up against was evil. Second, that it had a personality. I thought if evil could take the form of a personal being, then good—God—had to also. I realized God was someone I could personally address." In desperation, Allen turned to God to save him, and told God, "If you show yourself, I'll follow you on your terms for the rest of my life."

"Nobody showed up at my apartment with scripture verses or a Christian tract," Allen recalls. But as he prayed over the next two weeks, several things began happening. First, he recalls, "I repented for three days; I wept before the Lord in shame for what my life had amounted to." Allen then sensed God directing him to the Bible, something he once had little use for. "He let me know I was an infant spiritually and that I needed guidance and nourishment, and that if I didn't get refreshment I would wither and die." Since a Bible was nowhere to be found in his apartment, he went out and bought one, and still remembers the way he brought it home, full of expectation. "Page after page unfolded God's truth," he remembers of his reading, and through Christ, God brought Allen into what he calls a "love relationship."

Soon Allen was involved in an inner city ministry in Houston, which set the stage for the second dramatic chapter in his life, his U.S.-based mission, relief, and development work in Honduras, about which we will learn more in the next chapter. For now we will note that spiritual orientation has much to do with explaining who Allen is today. Our research shows us that the depth of his spirituality and the vividness of its reality exists among a greater proportion of Americans than many have thought.

We have concluded that the saints among us have a great deal to show us about the experience of spiritual reality. Not all of their stories compare in drama to Allen's, but the saints among us do consistently mention a strong awareness of God's presence. They seem more at home with prayer than the average believer. They have learned how faith can be more than a dry routine. Because such intimacy with the divine seems to set the stage for more mature faith and gives saints a "staying power" they would not otherwise have, we can gain much by exploring their experience in detail.

This may be especially important for the nineties. Historian of American religion Martin Marty has called the interest in prayer and spirituality over the last few years "an event of our era."[3] Repeated polls show that one American in three—33 percent—claims to have had a religious experience, a particularly powerful religious insight or awakening.[4] This substratum of religious experience has sometimes gone undernoticed or unexplored by sociologists, theologians, and even pastors. The saints among us remind us that religious affections are not to be overlooked as a reality or as a resource for change and growth.

It is true, it should be admitted, that in our experience-oriented times people sometimes put too much weight on subjective impressions; Americans are prone to base choices on what "feels" right, with little regard for the effect on others. And religious experience can be a mixed blessing. It can lead to self-absorption, privatism, and even arrogance. More than one figure in the history of the church has justified heresy or aberrant behavior by claiming divine "visitation."

Still, the saints among us, whatever their imperfections, have discovered that genuine closeness with God can lead to genuine holiness. We suggest several ways in which the saints among us have experienced a mature and authentic spirituality worth learning from.

Faith at work

First, a deep experience of God's love and presence involves everyday, not just mountaintop, experiences. Not all religious experiences, of course, are as dramatic as Allen's. As Thomas Merton writes, "After reading the lives of the saints and the experiences of the mystics, some people become convinced that the mystical life must be something like a Wagnerian opera. Tremendous things keep happening all the time. Every new motion of the Spirit is heralded by thunder and lightning. The heavens crack open and the soul sails upward out of the body into a burst of unearthly and splendid light."[5]

Instead, we found that the saints among us often maintain their spiritual orientation through long stretches of ordinary, mundane experiences. "I haven't had any major visions," one saint told us. "I feel God works daily in my life, I talk with him, and I feel he communicates with me, but in terms of a single instance where he 'wrote on the wall,' no." When asked if she has ever had a dramatic religious experience, Diane Wells of North Carolina reflects, "It's not so much in one particular experience, but in looking back over the years and seeing how situations have ended, you know it didn't happen by chance. More than anything really dramatic, I can see there was a plan there."

Indeed, while the vast majority of the saints participating in our follow-up interview admitted to having had some form of religious experience, some of the saints we talked with had trouble identifying a major "religious experience." We suspect that this is not because God is not real for them, but rather because they do not think of faith in terms of dramatic, sky-rending events. While the saints among us have found a deep spirituality, for many it is like that of the seventeenth-century monk, Brother Lawrence. In his spiritual classic, *The Practice of the Presence of God*, Lawrence was able to sense God as deeply while washing the pots and pans as in worship. "The time of business does not with me differ from the time of prayer; and in the noise and clatter of my kitchen, while several persons are at the same time calling for different things, I possess God in as great tranquility as if I were upon my knees at the blessed sacrament."[6] The saints among us have integrated work with worship, practicalities with prayer.

Saint among us Marie LaBreque is a good case in point. The retired correctional officer living in the tiny coastal town of Saco, Maine, was raised for a good portion of her childhood by Catholic nuns; she herself almost made a lifelong commitment to their order. But she came to believe that "you can keep up your religion" in the everyday world of marriage, children, and work. "Prayer doesn't mean you have to kneel and take a book and follow [printed] prayers. You can pray as you are starting the morning by offering your day and whatever little things that you do to God. . . . When I was working at the jail, I had seventeen miles to travel to work. As I drove I asked God for his help. It would give me patience for my work. If there was an inmate that needed help, I would try to understand, try to say the right thing to help him out."

David Hunt, a bus salesman in a small bedroom community in the rolling hills between Winston-Salem, High Point, and Thomasville, North Carolina, is another example. This is how he describes his spiritual angle on life: "[When I became a believer,] I didn't see a bright light. I don't say that some don't, but it wasn't that way for me. Faith was something I knew was missing from my life. Prayer and reading the Bible has brought me closer in my walk with Christ, closer to him."

However dramatic or mundane their experiences, whether faith comes with a flash of light and insight as it did with the Apostle Paul on the Damascus Road, with a heart "strangely warmed" as it did with Methodism's John Wesley, or as it did with the prophet Elijah, who heard a "still, small voice," the saints among us owe much of the remarkable character of their lives to their sense of God's reality at work in their lives. Many talk as though no day is so ordinary or commonplace but that God is in it. In driving to work, caring for sick loved ones, accomplishing the thousand and one tasks of daily life, they find a dimension of the transcendent that lends a special character to how they live and move and have their being.

Spirituality for the long haul

Second, the saints show that spirituality is not a one-time, once-for-all event, but more usually a process.

As David Hunt put it, "I expect growth. That's my goal. I have to have that faith that he's going to work with me. If I didn't believe that I'd be lost. The devil is out there, and if I'm not striving to get closer to Christ and develop that relationship then I'll be right back where I started from."

This awareness of having not "arrived" seems to keep the saints from smugness. Marie LaBreque, for example, quickly dismisses the idea that she has gotten holiness down pat. "I have a lot to do to become one of the saints." Most seem to realize that saintliness requires constant attention: regular reading of the Bible, praying, reflecting, worshiping, living. As educator Iris Cully notes, this growth "includes a conscious effort to develop. This statement goes counter to a viewpoint that holds the spiritual life to be spontaneous. In a sense it is spontaneous, in that the spirtual life is life lived entirely in the presence of God, and there is a necessary spontaneity in all good relationships. Beyond that, however, is the cultivation and expansion of a relationship."[7]

How did the saints get to be the way they are? We will say more about this in chapter 7. For now we will note that sainthood, even of the informal variety that we have been profiling, is no accident. It was not developed on automatic pilot. Spiritual commitment requires cultivation. Just as human relationships require intentional nurture through the years, so does a relationship to God develop with time and attention.

The place of prayer

Third, the saints among us show that prayer is important in saintliness. Prayer, we found, is vital for a large proportion of the saints among us. This is no surprise, given that one of the survey questions to which all saints responded affirmatively had to do with seeking God's will through prayer. What is more interesting is that when we asked in our follow-up mail interviews with several dozen, "Do you set aside time each day for prayer or meditation?" all but one of the score of respondents said yes. The saints among us obviously find prayer to be important enough for them to make it a regular part of their day.

What form does this prayer take? Sometimes it is a prayer of desperation. One saint among us told of a particularly stressful time in her marriage. "I was hurting so bad, things in my life were so crazy, I couldn't pray. I didn't know what to ask for. I felt so alone. So some nights I just sang [the child's song] 'Jesus Loves Me.' It was such a simple song, but I would sing that until I fell asleep. I knew [God] would honor that. The least little bit, he'll honor that."

Others mentioned repeating the Lord's Prayer or the Rosary (a series of prayers important in Catholic tradition). Interestingly, sociologist Margaret Poloma and George Gallup, Jr., found in a survey on varieties of prayer that only 22 percent of those who responded affirmatively to the question "Do you ever pray to God?" reported using a book of printed prayers on occasion. The vast majority (78 percent) did not.[8]

Some of the saints among us, however, used so-called rote prayers (known as vocal prayer in classical spiritual life teaching) in creative ways. One saint among us tries to pray an hour every day, using the Lord's Prayer. She says, "I pray the Lord's will be done in my life. That he watch over my family's finances, giving us the things we need. That he forgive me for anything I've done wrong, and protect me from temptation. I usually end the time praising God." One woman that said she prayed the Lord's Prayer every night, but would "pray it slowly; I don't go like a train to get through it."

The Paloma and Gallup survey showed that 95 percent of those surveyed who said they prayed do use their own words (conversational prayer). The things covered in such informal conversation with God included a number of themes, including asking for forgiveness, thanking God for blessings, seeking guidance on decisions, and asking God for material things. The saints among us manifested a similarly wide range of prayer topics.[9]

One saint we interviewed, Jeremy Longhurst, divided his prayer into several types. First, he says, he sees prayer as growing in the awareness of God's presence. "When I'm in the office or driving to work, I take time to thank the Lord for certain things. If I'm facing awkward situations, I lift those up to him. These prayers are brief, but I just try to be consistently aware of God's presence and his involvement in every day."

Second, he says, is his "more formalized time of prayer: I try to lift up major issues in my life. Or I pray for my wife, members of my family, friends, and for the community I live in. I also pray for the church I attend."

Third, he tries to take time "to lift up praise and thanks to Jesus." He notes that practical realities have their bearing on his practice of prayer. A recent move required him to spend three hours daily commuting, and his "formal times of prayer have really been eaten into. The good side of that is I'm really beginning to learn about walking through the day and trying to remain in contact with Jesus throughout. But the bad side is I'm not really getting the time I'd like to spend praying about major issues."

John Fafinski describes his daily prayer ritual in this way: "I do two things. First, I'll read the daily reading of Psalms in my prayer book [the Episcopal Book of Common Prayer]. Second, I use the Jesus Prayer [a prayer from the Eastern Orthodox tradition which involves repeating 'Lord Jesus, Son of the living God, have mercy on me a sinner.']. I'll take rosary beads, and I'll go around the rosary and I'll say the prayer on each bead, in a slow, meditative way. I feel a sense of the nearness of God. Plus I feel a sense that needs are being met. Things that are weighing on my heart are being lifted up to God without my having to go verbally through the details. It's being in communion in a deep way that goes beyond words. In intercession, if I know that something is going on—like if one of my kids is ill—instead of my having to name all the symptoms and 'Lord, heal her,' I just have a picture of her in my mind and I say, Lord, Jesus, have mercy. And it's as if I've lifted her up to the presence of Jesus. He knows far more about her condition than I could ever tell him."

Whatever the variety, the saints among us agree that prayer is significant for their faith and life. As one saint puts it, "It's vital for a relationship to the Lord—just like you can't have an earthly relationship with anybody without communicating with them. You have to share how you feel. And then there's time you listen, and you just feel a conviction from the Lord that what you are hearing is what he's leading you to do."

The communion of saints

Fourth, the saints among us have found a faith that is more than private, individualistic piety, but grows out of and feeds into relationships with others. The axiom of philosopher Alfred North Whitehead, that religion is what a person does with his solitude, far from exhausts the experience of the saints. For the great majority, faith is also a reality with great implications for relationships. This communal dimension finds its greatest expression through church. For many it also means participation in small groups, such as Bible studies, Sunday school classes, or informal networks.

One saint among us from New Mexico credits her involvement in a women's Bible study group with much spiritual growth. She says its "gets me with other women who have problems like I do. We can talk about it in that smaller group setting, touch on a lot of the things we maybe couldn't touch on with the whole congregation." She also notes that she and her husband "have always been supportive of Sunday School. That again is a small group where we have been helped very much as a couple by having books and studying parts of the Bible that pertain to marriage."

Jeremy Longhurst noted the way his church has made a big difference in his perspective. He went through a time of not being able to "sense any feeling or mental understanding inside that God loved me or cared about me. I would feel like I was just continually letting him down, not measuring up to his standards. It was only since finding my current church, where people could pray for me that God would really be able to affirm me, that I felt free of condemnation."

In this communal dimension the saints among us reflect, more than do the "rugged individualists" so idealized in our society, the biblical norm. In the New Testament, the writers make regular reference to the Greek word *koinonia*, variously translated into English as communion, fellowship, partnership, participation, or sharing. Jesus did seek out quiet places to pray alone, it is true, but he also stressed that faith is not a solitary exercise, but something that owes its genesis, nurture, and maturation to interaction with others. "A soul which remains alone," wrote sixteenth-century spiritual advisor John of the Cross, "is like a burning coal which is left by itself. It will grow colder rather than hotter." Whatever the place for solitude, Christian faith also stresses Jesus' words that "where two or three are gathered in my name, there am I with them."[10]

The saints, then, offer a good counterbalance to the cultural ethos of individualism which has infected the church. We have become an atomized society in which pursuit of what has been called the "untrammeled self" becomes more important than other values, such as family togetherness or participation in a faith community. Sociologist Robert Bellah and his cowriters point with concern to what they call our "language of radical individualism." They warn that "we find ourselves not independently of other people and institutions but through them. We never get to the bottom of our selves on our own. We discover who we are face to face and side by side with others in work, love, and learning. . . . We are not simply ends in ourselves, either as individuals or as a society. We are parts of a larger whole that we can neither forget nor imagine in our own image without paying a high price."[10]

As we shall see later, all this underscores the importance of relationships for growing in sanctity. Family, church, accountability relationships, and friendships all have a place.

A hunger for God

Fifth, the saints among us remind us that faith is more than concept, but can be a vivid reality. They are not content with the dry husks of a religion of mere habit or formalism. We found an openness to and a hunger for God in the vast majority of the saints among us with whom we talked. They would agree with Augustine's oft-quoted prayer, "You have made us restless until we find our rest in you."

In this, the saints reflect the long interest in spirituality that can be traced back to the initial intimacy of fellowship between Adam and Eve and God in the book of Genesis. And the saints would understand Paul the apostle's prayer for a congregation under his charge: "I pray that out of his glorious riches he may strengthen you with power through his Spirit in your inner being, so that Christ may dwell in your hearts through faith. And I pray that you, being rooted and established in love, may have power, together with all the saints, to grasp how wide and long and high and deep is the love of Christ, and to know this love that surpasses knowledge—that you may be filled to the measure of all the fullness of God" (Eph. 3:16–19, NIV). Many of the saints among us would understand the deep experiences of church history's mystics and contemplatives.

These spiritual longings and experiences, as we might expect, take many forms among the saints we encountered. Some experiences are even dramatic. However we might evaluate them, it is clear that people have such experiences and often find transformation in the wake of them, as becomes manifest in stories such as Allen's and in the accounts we now relate. One saint among us from Indiana, for example, tells of having forsaken the Christianity of her childhood when she was a young teenager. As a sixteen-year-old, she began searching again. "One evening, I went out in the front yard of our house, under a tree," she recounts. "I said to God, 'I need to know if you are real. I want to know that you're here, with me.'" And even though it was a completely calm evening, she says, "the tree began to shake—its branches, the whole thing *shook*. I knew then that he had not left me, that he cared for me."

Dotty Biros, whom we have already met, describes a time of intense searching for God at one point in her adult Christian life. Frustrated with the difficulty she had in approaching God in prayer, and curious about a friend's description of an experience of being "baptized in the Holy Spirit," Dotty remembers, "I was sitting by the fire-place in my living room, reading the Bible. I asked the Lord if there was a baptism in the Holy Spirit. I wanted something more in my praying if there was something more. My praying was awkward. I laid down on the floor, and the Lord took my hand, grasped it as in a handshake. I could feel the heat. Then a week or so later I noticed a difference in my prayer life. Words just started coming. I started thinking of people I hadn't thought of for a while, and I began praying for them."

Many of the saints' experiences of God's presence or in-tervention have this component of bringing empower-ment for helping another. Many of the saints point to experiences that they claim allow them to help others. Says a retired woman from New Mexico, "I had been counseling a gal who was a young Christian with a rough life and an alcoholic husband. The Lord sent her to me and me to her. She called and asked if she could come over. I told her I'd pray until she came because I sensed pain in her voice.

"As we talked, I sensed the Lord telling me that the

things she was telling me were not what was bothering her. I asked her, 'You were molested as a child, weren't you?' She let out a scream. 'Who told you? How did you know?' she asked. 'No one could have told you—I've told no one.' I said I didn't know, but the Lord did, and told me. I told her the Lord uses those of us who have gone through it to help deal with those who have." Sometimes, we found, the saints' religious experiences are less experiential. Their descriptions may draw heavily on the language of the theological tradition of the saints' upbringing, as this Southern Baptist's shows: "I realized that I was a sinner and that sin separated me from God. I repented and asked God's forgiveness. I asked him to be the Lord of my life. God saved me and sent his Holy Spirit to live in me and help me to live a life pleasing to him."

A faith that looks out as well as up

Finally, the saints among us, for all their spirituality, show that faith does not stop with warm feelings. This refutes the common view of some that deep spiritual concern inevitably involves a retreat into a cozy half-world of "God and me unendingly." Dostoyevski's character Fyodor Pavlovitch in *The Brothers Karamazov* captures these fears: "Here in this hermitage are twenty-five saints being saved. They look at one another and eat cabbages."[11] While much popular Christianity focuses inward and concentrates on spiritual feelings and glib promises that God will "meet our every need," the lives of the saints among us show a different side of the Christian faith. They demonstrate that spiritual awareness at its best can lead people to more, not less concern for the hurts and hungers of the wider world. This outward aspect of the saints' lives will form the basis of our next two chapters.

4

How a Saint Shows Compassion

This is the true joy in life, the being used for
a purpose recognized by yourself as a mighty one . . .
the being a force of Nature instead of a feverish selfish little clod
of ailments and grievances complaining that the world
will not devote itself to making you happy.
—Bernard Shaw[1]

In the last chapter we suggested that Allen Danforth's story did not end just with a dramatic conversion. He began working as a minister in an urban area of Houston. Then, he remembers, "out of the clear blue I was invited by a missionary evangelist to go to Ghana, West Africa. While there, I saw starvation and deprivation of a magnitude that I'd never comprehended. I was bombarded by one horror story after another." After a month, Allen boarded a plane for home. While he sat in his seat, he asked, "Lord, why did you ever send me here? What can anybody do? It's absolutely hopeless."

While Allen has the level-sounding voice of a businessman, he says that he next heard God telling him that he would be held "accountable" for what he had seen. "I got a knot in my stomach. I didn't have a vision, but in my mind's eye I could see myself standing all alone before Christ, accounting for my life as a Christian. That became on the plane the most real priority of my life. . . . When I got off the plane, I didn't know anything about being a missionary, but I knew that I could share a vision. I could tell people what I'd seen." There was little fanfare, but Allen gave a simple "yes" to the direction in which he sensed God taking him.

The sense of Allen's call was immediately tested. His wife suffered a brain hemorrhage during a church service within twenty-four hours of his return to the States. "The next three months we went into the valley of the shadow of death," Allen recalls, but he still managed to begin raising money for relief. "My wife went through two brain surgeries. The first one was an absolute failure and the doctors said she wouldn't make it through the night."

A second operation—and earnest prayers—brought her healing. Even through her illness, Allen could not forget completely the calling he felt to help the desparately poor people he had just seen. At the end of his wife's three-month ordeal and times when he didn't know one day of the week from another, times when he didn't remember whom he had called, Allen had raised over a million dollars of relief supplies for Ghana.

Even here Allen's story does not end. Because by 1983 Houston had become something of a gateway to Latin America, Allen got a visit from the Honduran Minister of Public Health, who had heard of his successes in raising money and supplies for relief. At the government's invitation Allen visited the country and began his life's relief, development, and missionary work in the slums and marginal rural areas of Honduras. From his base in the United States he works with Honduran pastors in providing medical care, food, and Bibles. He and his wife Dona have also adopted three Honduran children. Living in the foothills of the Ozarks in Little Rock, Arkansas, Allen is a little-known believer making a significant difference in the world. Indeed, his influence is felt not only by the thousands of Hondurans who benefit from his help, but also by the teams of dentists and short-term volunteers he frequently brings with him to Honduras, who come home changed and more compassionate from spending time among impoverished people.

Is Allen's commitment to other people unusual for the saints among us? Even if many of their stories are not as dramatic, we found that the saints are different from the norm not only in their spirituality, but in their expression of compassion. In what specific ways are they salt and light in a bland and dark world?

In chapter 2 we noted that saints claim to spend more time helping people in physical and emotional need than the rest of the population (73 percent of the saints among us versus 65 percent). It is interesting to break this down even further. When we look at those who answer only "strongly agree" to the twelve-item spiritual commitment scale, for example, the difference in these "supersaints" (7 percent of the U.S. population) is even more striking. Eighty-five percent of these exceptionally committed saints say they spend a good deal of time helping—twelve percentage points higher than the saints (those who answered "agree" or "strongly agree").

We also note that the further Americans move from the qualities of "sainthood" as defined by our questionnaire, the less likely they are to indicate involvement in charitable activities. For example, of those who answer "disagree" or "strongly disagree" to all twelve items on the spiritual commitment scale (a group that makes up 3 percent of the population), only 42 percent say they spend a good deal of time helping others.

The clear implication is that faith can be an influence

that motivates action. Christian tradition has always linked deep experience of God's love and presence with outgoing concern. "Faith by itself, if it is not accompanied by action, is dead," the apostle James wrote in the New Testament (Jas. 2:17, NIV). John also captured this connection when he wrote, "Dear friends, since God so loved us, we also ought to love one another" (1 John 4:11, NIV). And Paul said, "Be imitators of God, therefore, as dearly loved children, and live a life of love, just as Christ loved us" (Eph. 5:1–2, NIV).

We note that service to others can, of course, be born of a compulsive drive to win approval—from God or from others. People can serve out of an unhealthy sense that they thereby win their salvation, or out of a crippling compulsion never to consider their own needs for rest or replenishment. While doubtless some of the saints among us are not perfect on this score, we sensed, on the whole, a healthy faith at the core of their service. The motives for their giving, as we will now see, are in fact complex and varied.

Why saints care for others

When we asked the saints among us the specifics of their motivation for helping others, the answers ranged across several broad categories.

Some talked about their helping others as duty, like Tim Daniel, a Baptist pastor in North Carolina, who gave this reason for being loving: "Christ teaches love for the brethren and even your enemies. We are to be like Christ."

Dave Hunt of North Carolina likewise speaks of our obligation to others. He says that the Bible contains hard words against "taking advantage of poor people, ripping them off." He sees compassion modeled by Jesus in "all kinds of examples of how he lived his life. That's our duty. I'm not as well versed in the Bible as I should be, and hope I will be, but I know that [concern for the needy] is in the New Testament. We are told to help others. I can't quote you book, chapter, and verse, but I know we are told to do that."

Another spoke of his sense of serving others as growing out of gratitude. "God gave his Son out of love for me, which I don't deserve as a sinner." In the face of such a gift, the implication is, how can I not be less self-centered? Giving to others in this scenario is a byproduct of thankfulness.

Some of our saints mentioned the fulfillment they received as a reason. One retired college professor from Texas spoke of the "personal satisfaction: I kind of visualize myself as being a member of the kingdom of God. I see myself as God's junior partner in bringing about his kingdom on earth." Being part of something larger than he was gave him a sense of partnership and wholesomeness.

Some mentioned a sense of divine prompting or moving, just as Allen Danforth did above, or Maryann Deiber of New Mexico: On a "humongously busy" day as a clerk at the S&H Redemption Center where she worked, she remembers, she was counting S&H Green Stamp books when she looked up at a woman in line and felt led to ask her, "You're a Christian, aren't you?" The woman "began to bawl," Maryann remembers, and said, "I was beginning to wonder, because no one had asked me." Despite the crowd in the store that morning, Maryann was able to comfort her. "The Lord told me to talk to her about him. The woman's faith had been tested, and he used me. . . . He uses each one of us as fingers and toes and hands and mouths and ears and eyes through the Holy Spirit."

Some say the motivation for helping comes from deep spiritual experiences and are the spillover of growth and change within, like the saint from Massachusetts who spoke of God's love "overflowing" into her conversations. She also mentioned her concern about the abortion issue, and how when she writes newspaper editors and senators on behalf of her cause, "it's not a nudge that moves me, but a conviction I have. It's something I can't contain."

These varied spiritual motives confirm what Robert Wuthnow discovered in research compiled in his book *Acts of Compassion:* Many of the people he interviewed who are helping others, he notes, "resorted to biblical language to explain their motives for becoming involved in caring activities." One young man, for example, quoted 1 John 3:17: "If anyone has the world's goods and sees his brother in need, yet closes his heart against him, how does God's love abide in him?" He drew the conclusion from this verse that we simply are "commanded to love one another." Another, Wuthnow continues, "placed the emphasis less on duty and more on opportunity but still formulated her answer in religious terms: 'A good way to show your thankfulness to God is by helping others and seeing your own life as blessed.'" Still another pointed to Jesus as a role model because he told us, "Care for others and do not expect anything in return."[2]

Interestingly, Wuthnow cites a survey report, *Giving and Volunteering in the United States: Findings from a National Survey* done by the Gallup Organization and Independent Sector, Inc. (a philanthropic umbrella organization for charitable and religious groups) which found that "spiritual reasons" was among the top four responses given to an open-ended question that asked people how they came to give to various charities.[3] Referring to his own research, Wuthnow notes:

In my national survey people were asked to respond to a number of possible reasons for trying to be a person who is kind and caring. One of the statements read, "My religious beliefs teach me to be kind and caring." A majority (57 percent) said this was a major reason for them to be kind and caring. Another 26 percent selected it as a minor reason. Only 14 percent said it was not a reason for them to be kind and caring.[4]

All of this shows that we should not be surprised that the more spiritually committed are also the more socially conscious. Gallup research has found that persons who attended church in the last seven days are far more favorably disposed to church involvement in political activity than those who had not.[5] Far from religion being an "opiate of the people" that hinders compassion and caring, it can be a resource for tremendous social change.

On an individual level, one young adult saint from the Midwest exemplifies what we mean. He helps to lead a small group in his church, and helps some people he knows financially. He believes that what he is now able to give has roots in a spiritual transformation. "At this moment of my life there has been a certain amount of inner healing, so that I no longer seem as introspective as I once was. I'm finally able to reach out to people. I feel like I'm at the beginning of another season in life." The healing of inner conflicts set the stage for being concerned to be a healing presence for others.

Of course, there are many reasons other than purely spiritual why Americans, and specifically the saints among us, involve themselves in compassionate activity. While our initial survey did not specifically address motives for helping, we suspect that at least some of the saints among us have motives beyond the purely spiritual.

For example, many Americans trace their motivations

for helping to a certain understanding of human nature. They believe helping does not stem from thoughtful reflection as much as from an innate impulse within all humans, or perhaps from the fact that all are made in the "image of God" and have empathy for others "built in." Others would root concern for kind deeds in a general "civic virtue" that is part of the tradition of America. And no doubt some of our saints have partaken of the philosophical understanding called utilitarianism, which would stress the caring act's pragmatic value—either to society or to the psychological state of the helper. But because so many of the saints in our follow-up questionnaire could mention having done something to help another because they "believed it was in accordance with God's will," we conclude that religious faith is indeed a primary source of the saints' compassionate goodness.

Caring in America

What is the broader scene in which the saints among us do their deeds of compassion? Eighty million Americans are engaged in some kind of voluntary caring activities, according to Independent Sector.[6] Forty-five percent of respondents in a recent survey volunteer their time in some capacity, averaging 4.7 hours per week.[7]

The demographics seem to be changing for the average volunteer in America. We suggest there may be implications here for the saints among us. *Time* magazine, in a recent article on volunteerism, noted that the old stereotypes of housewives holding Chrismas bazaars, "the idle rich sponsoring benefits and the young selling cookies," don't do justice to the whole picture. In fact, the largest number of volunteers, according to a J.C. Penney survey, are between the ages of thirty-five and forty-nine.[8]

We suspect there is a connection here to new evidence

that the baby boomers (those born in the post-World War II era between 1946 and 1964) may be returning to church in increasing numbers.[9] We see a connection in that church members are more likely to be involved in charitable acts, especially through organized groups. (Almost half of church members did unpaid volunteer work in 1989, compared to only a third of nonmembers.)[10] It is also interesting to note that a recent Independent Sector/Gallup survey shows that those who attended religious services weekly "were clearly the most generous givers of both time and money, compared with all other groups," Regular churchgoers were "far more likely to give a higher percentage of their household income to charitable causes."[11]

As baby boomers return to church, then, we suspect they will find encouragement to give of themselves through volunteering. Also, as baby boomers join the ranks of volunteering, they find themselves turning to the spiritual resources offered by the churches many abandoned in their youth and young adulthood. Both factors could lead to an increase in the numbers of saints among us found among the baby boomers.

For now, however, we note that those between the ages of fifty and sixty-four, and, even more so, those over sixty-five, are more likely to be saints among us, which suggests they are still more likely to be involved in acts of compassion. Among the baby boomers (aged 22–42 years at the time of the saints among us survey), a full 10 percent are saints among us, less than the 13 percent overall percentage, but still a significant group.

The shape of help

In *Acts of Compassion*, Wuthnow observes that Americans are involved in a wide range of helping activities.

They bake cookies for local elementary schools, visit people in nursing homes, staff crisis pregnancy hotlines, and serve on the boards of nonprofit organizations. Approximately 31 million people do volunteer work each year for their churches or synagogues.[12]

The saints among us, we found, likewise mentioned a variety of helping acts. One saint told of hearing that a friend was about to be evicted from her apartment, so he volunteered to pay her rent. Others helped victims of cancer, through practical help, prayer, or both. Some went out of their way to visit the hospitalized, volunteered heavily in church programs such as Sunday school, lent a listening ear to a troubled relative, and gave money to a host of charitable causes, from Robert Schuller's Hour of Power television broadcast to relief organizations serving the world's poor. A number did their work through voluntary organizations such as churches, food pantries, or civic groups such as the Lions Club. Some saw their mission in terms of changing social structures by writing letters, or other forms of public persuasion and influence.

Whatever the forms of their service, we believe that the saints among us are particulary significant during a time when society is growing more interested in volunteering. They are important not only for the good they do, but also for the models they provide. The *Time* story mentioned above quoted Kenneth Adams, executive director of New York Cares, a sort of charitable clearinghouse for young urban professionals that had, at the time of the article's writing, recruited six hundred young volunteers to tutor dropouts, serve in soup kitchens, renovate housing, and visit the elderly. He said, "We're trying to break the cycle of you get up, you go to work, step over a homeless person on the way to the subway, go to the gym, go to the sushi bar, go home and fall asleep."[13] The saints provide good starting places for those ready to begin the process of breaking that cycle.

U.S. News & World Report carried a similar story a few years ago. "Just when the evidence suggests that traditional American idealism is languishing," it noted, "countervailing signs are cropping up. After the Me Decade and the Gimme Decade, many Americans are starting to feel uncomfortable with the unbridled pursuit of their private interests and are volunteering for a widening array of community-service activities."[14] There is a great reserve or residue of idealism that may simply need nudging, or modeling, to flourish.

Those who help others, however, may need to be encouraged to see also the larger, societal dimensions of compassion. Robert Wuthnow argues that many volunteers in America already see the problems of society as "systemic, going beyond the misfortunes of particular individuals."[15] They recognize that problems such as homelessness, crime, and inner-city problems need more than individual action, but rather large-scale social reform. "Many problems," Wuthnow argues, "require huge expenditures of public money or legislative action or the coercive powers of government in addition to simple acts of kindness."[16] The church and other institutions need, therefore, to encourage both individual acts of kindness and longer-term efforts to change structures.

Back to the source

The saints among us, we hasten to add, are essential to society not just for their modeling of self-giving, but also for the resources for well doing they draw on. Because their impulse to do good is rooted in more than trends or civic duty, they have a staying power for service that those caught up in the "new volunteerism" may soon need to grasp.

The gospels provide a good example of the interlocking relationship of spiritual resources and sustained service. Jesus, we learn in Mark 1:32–34, was in Capernaum of Galilee, when, after a rigorous day of healing and teaching, the "whole town gathered at the door, and Jesus healed many who had various diseases." We learn immediately in the next verse, however, that "very early in the morning, while it was still dark, Jesus got up, left the house and went off to a solitary place, where he prayed" (Mark 1:35, NIV). Even Jesus did not attempt a life of unremitting activism, but knew the value of a rhythm of service and renewal, speaking and silence, giving and receiving.

While spirituality can be an escape into privatism, an effort to avoid painful personal or social conflicts, activism also holds the danger of becoming activity without adequate grounding. Compassionate people can "burn out" if they do not guard the inner resources, the wellsprings of spiritual renewal, from which service must flow. It is here that the saints can help. Faith seems to be a necessary foundation source for the the good deeds that so distinguish their lives. Faith may ultimately be a necessary ingredient for a lifestyle of true self-sacrifice.

Furthermore, a cultivation of the inner life is necessary to keep love from being superficial or shallow, and to give it richness and depth. Thomas Merton once observed, "Music is pleasing not only because of the sound that is in it: without the alternation of sound and silence there would be no rhythm." It is that way with our service and spirituality, he said. "If we have no silence, God is not heard in our music. If we have no rest, God does not bless our work. If we twist our lives out of shape in order to fill every corner of them with action and experience, God will silently withdraw from our hearts and leave us empty."[17]

It is no accident that Jesus, in answering a questioner who wondered what the greatest commandment was, first replied, "'Love the Lord your God with all your heart and with all your soul and with all your mind.' This is the first and greatest commandment." Only then did he conclude, "And the second is like it: 'Love your neighbor as yourself'" (Matt. 22:37–39, NIV).

A "cut-flower civilization"?

The connection between faith and deeds, between spirituality and compassion, has societal dimensions, not just personal ones. The great philosopher of religion Elton Trueblood noted the role of religious faith in society when he wrote, "The terrible danger of our time consists in the fact that ours is a *cut-flower civilization.* Beautiful as cut flowers may be, and much as we may use our ingenuity to keep them looking fresh for a while, they will eventually die, and they die because they are severed from their sustaining roots. We are trying to maintain the dignity of the individual apart from the deep faith that every man is made in God's image and is therefore precious in God's eyes."[18] We believe the saints among us are in touch with a transcendent dimension that more than many people realize, may be the hope of civilization.

Nancy Longhurst, a young woman in her twenties, is one saint who shows this connection through a simple but significant story. She was in church one morning when a couple who worked with children with disabilities and profound retardation stood to talk about their work. "I remember clearly sitting in the church," she says, "and feeling strongly that that is what I should do, even though I had never done it before and was a bit afraid of people with disabilities." Living largely off savings, she spent the next year in the couple's household. Through being with them and watching how they treated the children they cared for, she says, "seeing how their philosophy was always to approach a child with love, I learned to care for people. I learned that that has to be at the heart of this field: to serve people as Christ would serve."

Historian Glenn Tinder has put Nancy's discovery in more academic terms to suggest something similar. Ultimately, he argues, "good customs and habits need spiritual grounds, and if those are lacking, they will gradually, or perhaps suddenly in some crisis, crumble." We cannot think that there are no societal implications from the secularization our culture has experienced in recent decades, he believes. We wrongly assume that we can continue to treasure "the life and welfare, the civil rights and politcial authority, of every person without believing in a God who renders such attitudes and conduct compelling." Tinder asks, "To what extent are we now living on moral savings accumulated over many centuries but no longer being replenished? To what extent are those savings already severely depleted?"[19]

If the dominant message we get from the culture is that *our* needs, *our* ambitions, *our* self-fashioned goals for life are all that matters, we need the saints among us to remind us differently. While we are told that we have a right to live for ourselves, buy what satisfies our whims, and think little about God or others, the saints model something else. By their convictions and by their behavior they can remind us how to live, and where to find the resources to act on our higher impulses, as a society and as members of society.

5

Everyday Goodness

In the realm of the Spirit we soon discover that the real issues are found in the tiny, insignificant corners of life. Our infatuation with the "big deal" has blinded us to this fact.
—Richard Foster[1]

Like musicians, painters, poets, [saints] are human beings but obsessed ones. They are obsessed by goodness and by God as Michelangelo was obsessed by line and form, as Shakespeare was bewitched by language, Beethoven by sound. And like other genuises they used mortal means to contrive their masterpieces.
—Phyllis McGinley[2]

What kind of influence do the saints have among their circle of daily acquaintances?

Forty-year-old Laura Cooper tells a story that gives a glimpse. She works at the same sales office in the Midwest industrial and residential town as John Fafinski (whom we met earlier), and is his wife's sister. John is not just her colleague and brother-in-law, however. Laura says that more than anyone, John was "instrumental in leading me to the Lord."

It was not eloquent, persuasive speeches that did it. She says that her transformation from skeptic to a believer had mostly to do with who John *was*, and not so much the couple of times he tried to talk to her about his faith, which only made her defensive.

A turning point was this incident she recounts: One morning John took a call that came for her. It was a caller she wanted to avoid. "Tell him I'm not here," she told

John. John did so, but the fact that he had told even a small lie began to trouble him. She remembers, "John came back later and told me how bad he felt for having lied. He told me he had confessed to the Lord his sin of lying, and that he could no longer lie for me."

At that point she began to realize that there was something unusual about the character of John's life. "I wasn't one to lie a great deal, but I realized he had a level of integrity that was different. As we talked about it, I came to a new understanding about his beliefs and his convictions about sin. It made a big difference." It wasn't his "preaching" that moved her, she recalls, but him. And as she continued to watch John, she became impressed at how he treated his wife, who was her sister. "I had never seen a man more devoted to his wife than John. When I saw their relationship, I often said I wish I had what they had. And I knew instinctively the Lord was in their life and that was the reason for their special relationship. I think I knew I wanted the [inner] peace he had."

It wasn't long before Laura began going to church. Gradually, she came to a point at which she felt she could trust the Lord and commit herself to the God she had reacted to so defensively before.

Another colleague of John's, Laura Matthieu, has a different perspective. While she also credits John in helping to lead her from unbelief to faith, she felt his influence in a different way. For her, it was John's convictions that struck her. She felt that some Christians she had been around "hid" their faith or acted awkward about it. "But I remember walking into John's office to find him praying—head bowed, eyes closed, as he gave thanks for his lunch. It wasn't awkward." When questions of personal belief came up, John "made it sound so believable." When a time of crisis hit Laura, she needed a caring person and turned to John. "At that moment he stepped in in a gentle way and shared the gospel."

It would leave a wrong impression to imply that John is pushy with his beliefs. He notes that over the years a "hard sell" approach to evangelism has never worked for him. "Instead, I've found that if I just make sure that the fruit of the Spirit [to echo the New Testament's imagery for character] is evident in my life, if I maintain peace and composure when things are going nuts and other people are losing it, I find that much more effective. For me it's a matter of allowing the Spirit to speak through your behavior. I think that opens a door to where the person will come to you and ask. Then you can tell the reason for the faith you have. To me that is so much better than trying to knock down doors on your own power."

We have suggested that the lives of the saints among us are different, in both their inward spirituality and their social compassion. We also find a difference in their day-to-day relationships, with people they live with and know on a daily basis. As best as we were able to ascertain, their faith influences how they act among family, friends, and neighbors. Virtues such as forgiveness and humility seem to be in operation to a significant degree. While we may picture sanctity as a commodity of the prayer closet or study, it also finds its test in the kitchen, or along the apartment hallway or front yard fence where people meet neighbors.

Dotty Biros, whom we met at the beginning of this book, spoke in this way of the changes that growing faith brought to her relationships with others. "When I got angry before, I always justified the anger. 'They were wrong, they treated me bad,' I'd say to myself, and I'd hang on to that. But I felt that that has destroyed me so much. Now when I can't pray for the anger to go away, I pray that God would help supply the desire to pray that way. I say, 'Help me to let go of this, to desire not to be angry.'"

The late-sixteenth-century spiritual writer Francis de Sales says that the great virtues and small kindnesses are like sugar and salt. For all that sugar may have a more exquisite taste, we use it less frequently. Salt, on the other hand, is found everywhere. The great virtues, the lofty aspirations, he concluded, are a rare occurrence, while the moment-by-moment ways in which we relate to others for our daily service are perhaps of even greater significance than the mighty deeds.

We found that the saints among us do indeed exercise much of their influence in the ordinary, everyday ways in which they relate and choose not to relate. They are like Dorcas in the New Testament, willing to make "coats and garments for the widows" (Acts 9:39), working good in the small things, in the smiles, in the handshakes, in their reactions to hostility and hurt. Fénelon writes, "It is not elevation of the spirit to feel contempt for small things. It is, on the contrary, because of too narrow points of view that we consider as little what has such far reaching consequences."[3]

One of the authors of this book was discussing with a couple of friends the everydayness of the saints' influence. One of the friends, a college professor, confessed, "Hearing this helps me remember that the little things I do count for something—the things I do almost on the run, like having students over to my house. All this helps me not get weary in well-doing. It reminds me of the significance of the things I'm tempted to think might be trivial." The other friend, a writer and radio show host, reflected, "I was thinking about the things people have done for me through my life that meant the most to me. I realized it was the almost unplanned, tiny touches—the small gifts, like someone picking up a phone to ask how I'm doing—that mattered the most. Often it was the Holy Spirit prompting them to do the small thing, but it was the right thing at the right time, and it had great significance."

God has chosen "things of little strength and small repute . . . to explode the pretensions of the things that are" (1 Cor. 1:28, J.B. Phillips translation).

Forgiven to forgive

Another aspect of daily relating we noticed in the saints among us had to do with a forgiving spirit. This factor shows up in our survey with a question about response to those who cause hurt. All of the saints among us, of course, answered either "agree" or "strongly agree" to the statement on the twelve-item survey, "God gives me the strength, that I would otherwise not have, to forgive people who have hurt me deeply."

In addition, saints among us are more likely than the general population to say they believe it is important to forgive people who hurt them deeply (98 versus 87 percent). They are not ones, in other words, who tend to seek revenge or live with seething hostility. The confirmed "nonsaints," those who disagreed with all twelve spiritual commitment survey questions, are dramatically less likely to be forgiving.

We suggest that this "forgiveness factor" makes the saints more constructive, reconciling members of society. Rather than nursing hurts and expending energy on scheming revenge, they are more likely to move on, and, in some cases, actually effect reconciliation. One saint, for example, when asked if she had gone out of her way in the last twenty-four hours to do something because she believed it was in accordance with God's will, wrote, "I made a telephone call to a person with whom I have had difficulty keeping a good relationship. It did help."

Another saint, Jim Volovlek, a factory worker from Michigan, tells this story: "Someone in my church had spread rumors about my being a social drinker. I ended up losing my position as a church board member because of it. The church was dividing because of the war between this woman and me. But God confronted both of us. We didn't seek counseling. We had a [worship] service at our church where I went down to the altar to pray about it and she went down to the altar at the same time. We finally settled it there. We both had a true experience of forgiveness toward each other."

Can we know, however, that saints are truly more likely to forgive when actually wronged? Can we rely on their own assessment that they work at forgiveness? In recent research Margaret Poloma and George Gallup, Jr., found that people who reported that religion was "very important" to them were more likely to respond in positive ways to being hurt (forgiving, discussing the matter to bring feelings out into the open, praying for the person) as opposed to negative responses (such as seeking revenge).[4] Because the saints among us can be assumed to be heavily represented in the group who say religion is very important, we can suggest that the Poloma/Gallup finding supports our conclusion about the saints among us.

Poloma and Gallup also found that those who engage in prayer regularly, such as our saints do, are for the most part more likely to respond in a healthy manner when wronged. They conclude, "Prayer is the single most important factor in explaining why some persons are better able than others to forgive those who have wronged them."[5]

John Fafinski, whom we met earlier in this chapter, certainly seems to support the presence of forgiveness among our saints when he reflects on how he tries to forgive and why. "I always remember all that I've been forgiven of. I think of my life before I knew the Lord and even after I knew him, all the things I've done and all the hurt I've caused. And he has always forgiven me. How can I not forgive? I've come to realize that when I'm holding a grudge, I'm not acting as God wants. I'm not extending the forgiveness that he's extended to me. I try to work on that. It's harder for me to keep up animosity now. When I do that I feel so bad about it that it's better to forgive and to repair the relationship, rather than allow that to go on."

In this, the saints among us model the spirit and practice of Jesus, who, even on the cross of crucifixion, prayed, "Father, forgive them, for they know not what they do." The saints live the sentiment of the petition of the Lord's Prayer: "Forgive us our trespasses, as we forgive those who trespass against us." They also seem to have taken to heart the New Testament's many injunctions to "bear with each other and forgive whatever grievances you may have against one another. Forgive as the Lord forgave you" (Col. 3:13, NIV).

A holy hiddenness

The saints, we found, also bring to their relationships a note of humility. John, for example, is described by friends as having a true willingness to listen to others. He has a gentleness that could be mistaken for shyness, and a self-effacing manner. He also knows that whole areas of his relationships with others still need work. "There are occasions when I hold grudges, like when I fight with my wife," he confesses. "The way I express it—which is really despicable—is to become silent. I give her the silent treatment. I'm very abrupt and won't smile. I'm working on that."

The saints among us with whom we talked seem to realize that humility should be a consequence and outgrowth of faith. Many undoubtedly remember the words of the apostle Paul to "do nothing out of selfish ambition or vain conceit, but in humility consider others better than yourselves" (Phil. 2:3, NIV). There is indeed a long tradition of Christian spirituality and practice that emphasizes the corrosive effects on relationships that comes from pride (one of the Roman Catholic church's traditional "seven deadly sins"). Thomas á Kempis' *The Imitation of Christ* is a good example of this emphasis on humility. So is William Law's *A Serious Call to a Devout and Holy Life*, which had a dramatic impact upon eighteenth-century England. Here is how he describes humility: "Condescend to all the weaknesses and infirmities of your fellow-creatures, cover their frailties, love their excellencies, encourage their virtues, relieve their wants, rejoice in their prosperities, [be] compassionate in their distress, receive their friendship, overlook their unkindness, forgive their malice, be a servant of servants, and condescend to do the lowest of offices to the lowest of mankind."[6]

This attitude, of course, seems foreign in our current climate of "looking out for number one." The saints' willingness to forgive, not to be pushy, not to be filled with their own self-importance is a good reminder of how faith should look when truly lived.

The difference God makes

The saints among us seem to see daily relationships in light of their spiritual commitment. They frequently mention God's help as they work on their relationships with others, crediting him with giving them patience or staying power to keep important relationships strong. North Carolinian Dave Hunt's marriage has become stronger, for example, thanks to God's intervention. "That's not to say my wife and I haven't had problems," he says. But we view them differently now. We don't accept all the burden as to what we are going to do. We ask, how is Christ going to get us out of it? What do we need to do as Christians to work through it?"

Another saint described the help her faith gives her in relating to her family and the schoolchildren she teaches: "I try to see others as God sees them and love them in spite of their faults. . . . I think when you walk with the Lord for a long time, doing and saying things he would want you to do is just second nature."

The daily actions of the saints among us, far from being irrelevant, are the place where their faith is played out most of the time. There is a this-worldly aspect to their religion that keeps the saints from being so "heavenly minded they are of no earthly good." "Who is wise and understanding among you?" asked one writer in the early church. "Let him show it by his good life, by deeds done in the humility that comes from wisdom" (Jas. 3:13, NIV).

Evelyn Underhill, a writer of our own century, notes, "We are the agents of the Creative Spirit in this world. Real advance in the spiritual life, then, means accepting this vocation with all it involves. Not merely turning over the pages of an engineering magazine and enjoying the pictures, but putting on overalls and getting on with the job. The real spiritual life must be horizontal as well as vertical."[7]

6

A Different Kind of Joy

From silly devotions and from sour-faced saints,
good Lord, deliver us.
—Teresa of Avila[1]

Religious rapture, moral enthusiasm, ontological wonder,
cosmic emotion, are all unifying states of mind,
in which the sand and grit of the selfhood incline to disappear,
and tenderness to rule.
—William James[2]

The chief end of man is to glorify God and enjoy him forever.
—Westminster Shorter Catechism

One of the first things you notice about someone we'll call Tom Davies is his speech. The bouyant 25-year-old marketing manager of a medical book publisher based in Chicago has not lived in the United States long enough to have lost his British accent. But even more striking than the way he talks is what he says when he explains the changes he experienced in his outlook on life when he became a Christian several years ago.

"The person I was before was consumed with wanting to earn a lot of money. I was very ambitious." His former classmates back in England still pursue those goals. "They seem to be happy, on the outside," he observes. "They're enjoying flourishing careers. But when I look at how I'd end up in the long term by following that route, I see that I'd hit my fifties and become disillusioned. I would realize that there had to be more to life. I think my having come to Christ will give me a whole new balance and purpose in the long term, which will make me a whole lot happier."

However, Tom Davies also says that becoming a Christian has not made his life a "bed of roses." He even says that in the short term, "my Christian faith has made me sadder in some ways. I find my faith leading me to confront some things—big psychological and emotional issues—that people are normally able to bury. Facing those issues can be a painful experience, especially for someone like me, who spent a lot of life feeling unaffirmed."

His confrontation of unresolved personal issues sometimes has even led to him feeling "down in the dumps, lonely, and somewhat depressed." He reflects, "Most of the guys I know cover all that up by doing well in their jobs and dating an attractive person. But I decided that I'm not going to do that; that I'm going to try to get to the root of my emotional needs and allow God to affirm me." In the past several months, Tom believes he has experienced a "a breakthrough in that area. I feel happier now than I probably have in my entire life. I suddenly have a lovely sense that God has turned around to me and said, 'Hey, I like you.'"

The saints among us as a group, we found, tend to share Tom's strong, though certainly not superficial, sense that life is fuller, happier, and more satisfying because of faith. The saints in our survey consistently characterized themselves as "very happy." Ninety-three percent said they were very happy, compared to 86 percent of the rest of Americans. This difference was underscored in an even more dramatic way in 1981: a similar survey, using seven questions about faith and spiritual life, showed that 68 percent of those who answered "completely true" to the seven statements about faith and spiritual life answered affirmatively to the statement "I am very happy." In contrast, only 30 percent of those who answered "completely untrue" to all seven questions could say they were "very happy."[3]

Interestingly, a Gallup survey in 1989 showed that those who are the most enthusiastic about religion are also more likely to be happy, less likely to get depressed, and less likely to have a lot of stress in their lives. Those who agreed strongly with the statements, "You receive comfort and support from your religious beliefs," and "Your religious faith is the most important influence in your life" were also more likely to agree strongly with a series of statements about personal optimism, happiness, and feelings of closeness to family.[4] The spiritually committed, in other words, are far more likely to see their lives as satisfying and happy. What is the source of that happiness?

When it comes to the saints among us, some might suggest that this satisfaction has roots in the saints' involvement in helping others. While Tom and other saints we talked with said that practicing their faith made their lives seem more "worthwhile," data from sociologist Robert Wuthnow suggests that a lifestyle of helping others alone does not account for greater joy and happiness. His survey of Americans found that those who receive a sense of fulfillment from helping others "are not demonstrably happier and do not have higher self-esteem, taking other things into account, than people who do not help others and do not find fulfillment from this source."[5] The picture is more complicated, therefore, and we must look to other areas also for understanding the saints' greater happiness.

Where happiness is found

We believe that our research points to religious faith and practice as a primary source of happiness for the saints among us. Later we will explore Tom's further reflections on where deep-seated happiness is found, observations in turn corroborated by the testimony of a number of the saints we interviewed. For now we will note that the saints we interviewed all saw belief in God and other aspects of religious faith as a primary source of satisfaction in life.

There is a common societal view, of course, that suggests that religion dampens joy or robs people of joy, a perennial stereotypical belief that religious faith is stifling and oppressive. Deeply religious people have often been portrayed in literature and in modern entertainment media as gloomy, narrow souls, so that few in society associate faith with expansive joy. A friend of one of the authors tells of a neighbor who is "dour and pietistic." Most of us know people who, for all their religion, are not a pleasure to be around.

However, we sensed in the saints we talked with, not pious stuffiness, but a constant and remarkable sense of the goodness of life and the joy of living, sometimes even in the midst of personal reversals or great stresses. Granted, their reserve may sometimes hide the deep currents of inner satisfaction, but they seem, for the most part, to be examples of Jesus' statement in John's gospel that "I have come that they may have life, and have it to the full" (John 10:10, NIV).

Popular author Keith Miller tells of a time of personal crisis when he committed his life to God in a profound way and discovered the connection between joy and the life of faith. "Something came into my life that day," he writes, "which has never left. There wasn't any ringing of bells or flashing of lights or visions; but it was a deep intuitive realization of what it is God wants from a [person], which I had never known before. And the peace which came with this understanding was not an experience in itself, but was rather a cessation of the conflict of a lifetime. . . . I knew to the core of my soul that I had somehow made personal contact with the very Meaning of Life."[6]

Many persons in recent history, in a variety of contexts, have made the association between happiness and the life of faith. For example, Blaise Pascal, the seventeenth-century French scientist and religious philosopher, went so far as to suggest that "it is quite certain that there is no good without the knowledge of God; that the closer one comes, the happier one is, and the further away one goes, the more unhappy one is."[7] He argued that "there are three kinds of people: those who have sought God and found him, and these are reasonable and happy; those who seek God and have not yet found him, and these are reasonable and unhappy; and those who neither seek God nor find him, and these are unreasonable and unhappy."[8]

William James, the experimental pyschologist and philosopher of the nineteenth and early twentieth centuries, likewise noted a connection between religion and happiness. He observed one of the universal "features" of saintliness to be "an immense elation and freedom, as the outlines of the confining selfhood melt down."[9] He spoke of the "transition from tenseness, self-responsibility, and worry, to equanimity, receptivity, and peace" as "the most wonderful of all those shiftings of inner equilibrium, those changes of the personal centre of energy, which I have analyzed so often," and noted the relationship to faith. "The chief wonder of it is that it so often comes about, not by doing, but by simply relaxing and throwing the burden down. This abandonment of self-responsibility seems to be the fundamental act in specifically religious, as distinguished from moral practice."[10]

Varieties of happiness

With issues such as these in the background, we approached the saints among us curious about the ways in which their faith has made them happier. Their answers were varied.

First, a number mentioned a conviction that God's care was making a significant difference in their outlook upon life. Tom talked about it as a sense of sudden realization that God "liked" him. Another saint said that she believed that "God loves us all and wants our happiness." Another: "Through the Holy Spirit, God and Jesus have shown me that I am a special person no matter what."

We found that a number expressly mentioned experiencing God's caring presence during times of crisis. More than one alluded to the verse in the New Testament that says "we know that in all things God works for the good of those who love him" (Rom. 8:28, NIV). One elderly saint said, "I don't believe God causes bad things to happen to people, but I have a strong belief that he uses events in our lives to some good." One of our saints, a fifty-seven-year-old Nebraskan grandmother with multiple sclerosis and severe visual impairment, said faith makes her life "more fulfilled. . . . I always have the Lord to talk to. When I get in trouble I say my prayers. God's always there."

While finding God in the midst of a crisis has sometimes been pilloried as "foxhole religion," or religion as a "crutch," we found the saints' view of God generally more mature than that. They seem instead to have discovered, as Paul the apostle did, "the secret of being content in any and every situation" (Phil. 4:12, NIV). They have discovered with Monica Furlong that "maturity . . . seems to lie in the discovery that happiness and circumstances don't have all that much to do with each other; that happiness is more a matter of choice and habit than we suppose, and less dependent upon the accident of circumstances."[11]

With the saints among us, this "habit of happiness" sometimes has to do with a belief that God is greater than circumstances, more powerful than the things that strike fear. A number spoke of God's ability to prevail, like one saint who believed that God could be trusted to give his followers "an inner peace, especially when things get really bad and you are helpless to do anything." One said that now "I'm not as quick to worry. If I have a problem I leave it in the hands of God." Another recalled that before she came to a place of "knowing God loves me and that he's my heavenly Father, when I had a problem I always turned to people, not to God. Now I'm not so desperate to call someone on the phone to hear them say, 'You're okay.' I still turn to people to pray for me, but now I know God can help too. When I get desperate, I go to church."

Several spoke of experiencing God's forgiveness as giving them a feeling of being given a new start. "Jesus has forgiven me of my sins. It lifted a load off me and changed my life." Others spoke of the "assurance of salvation." Faith helped another "in understanding the past part of my life and putting it in proper perspective, and in knowing that life does work out and there is eternity of peace to come."

Second, the saints believe that faith makes a difference in their attitude toward the future. As Tom puts it, "Faith has given me a greater sense of hope than I can imagine anybody having who is not a Christian. I am excited about what the Lord is going to do in my relationship with him and in my marriage, and in my life, my vocation. It makes me very excited for the future. When I look at some of my friends, who are still chasing being promoted to branch manager, or worrying about making enough to get a five-bedroom detached house, I see that they don't seem to have much passion for the future."

Part of this sense of expectation and trust when facing the future may stem from the saints' tendency to view their lives as "guided" by the Holy Spirit and scripture. A number mentioned both a general awareness of such guidance and specific instances where God gave explicit direction. Said one saint of her times of seeking God's guidance, "Prayer is how you communicate with the Lord. And then there's a time when you listen, and you feel a conviction from the Lord that a certain course of action is what he's leading you to do. In any decision, I want to feel that that's what the Lord wants me to do. For the Christian, there's nothing more miserable than being out of the Lord's will." This confidence in God's involvement in their lives gave many saints a sense of anticipation for the future.

For many of our saints this expectancy was related to understandings of the afterlife. Seven out of ten Americans believe in life after death,[12] but many of the saints we questioned are not only convinced of the existence of a life to come, they positively look foward to it. They speak of "eternal life in heaven" and the promise of "seeing the Lord's face" as one of the rewards of believing. This conviction and certainty about what lies beyond death can lend great courage to life. One retired schoolteacher from Kentucky said, "When I die I'll be in heaven with God the Father, Jesus Christ our Lord and Savior, and the Holy Spirit—and loved ones who have gone on before."

The conviction of the saints about the afterlife may have special relevance to a society beginning to become aware again of the inescapability of mortality. "All of a sudden," writes *Washington Post* reporter Michael Specter, "a generation taught first to trust nobody over thirty, and then to seek fulfillment through accumulated goods, has stumbled over the notion of its eventual demise." Baby boomers and yuppies, says Specter, are experiencing their first "real intimations of mortality," fueling a growing multibillion-dollar funeral arrangement business.[13] The saints' tendency to view death with the hope of life to come can model something attractive and valuable in a secular society looking for certainty.

Third, the saints say that religious faith led them to an approach to life oriented toward doing good, toward participating in a cause beyond themselves. Tom notes how his religious commitment has given him a sense of being involved in and doing something "worthwhile." "One of the things that got me to become a Christian was looking at people who were Christians and were spending their lives doing things that the world thought stupid—and they seemed far happier!" Tom mentioned Mother Teresa of Calcutta as an example. "She's not married, she's not rich, she's got no real status, yet everyone who meets her seems to think she's the happiest person around. For me to be able to do something even at work that encourages someone, to do something that seems to make other people feel good, gives me a sense of happiness."

Writer Philip Yancey once made a fascinating observation about the source of fulfillment. He noted that in his career as a writer and journalist he has interviewed a wide range of people, whom he divides roughly into two types: the stars and the servants. For the stars—NFL football greats, famous authors, TV personalities—he shows sympathy. These "idols," he says, "are as miserable a group of people as I have ever met." They appear to have more troubled marriages, tormented psyches, and incurable self-doubts than most. But the servants, relief workers in Bangladesh or Ph.D.'s scattered through the jungles of South America translating the Bible into obscure languages are the favored ones. "I was prepared to honor and admire these servants, to uphold them as inspiring examples. I was not, however, prepared to envy them. But as I now reflect on the two groups, stars and servants, the servants clearly emerge as the favored ones, the graced ones. They work for low pay, long hours, and no applause, 'wasting' their talents among the poor and uneducated. But somehow, in the process of losing their lives, they have found them."[14]

The way to happiness

"The quest for serenity is a phenomenon of our times," says one writer.[15] For all the burgeoning interest in spirituality and inner peace, however, people still try to escape from restlessness in a well-filled clothes closet or an elaborate house. Even in the church people are tempted to internalize standards of happiness from society, which says that happiness is found in externals—the car you drive, your health, your neighborhood. The saints among us show the truth of C. S. Lewis's observation that people "are not sufficient for their own bliss." The simple yet profound lives of the people we have talked with convince us that the character in French novelist Leon Bloy's *The Woman Who Was Poor* was right: "There is only one unhappiness, and that is not to be one of the saints." A society that seems almost frantic at times not to miss out on the "best" things in life needs to look in an unexpected place: the simple but grace-filled lives of the everyday saints who have found authentic satisfaction in surprising places.

7

Becoming a Saint

I believe . . . in the communion of saints.
—Apostles' Creed

What is the Church but the congregation of all saints?
—Bishop Nicetas (fifth century)[1]

"We're not meant to be alone," one of our saints, a retired nurse from Nashville, reflects. "I think we're meant to support one another, to be like trees in a forest, whose roots intertwine and hold each other up." Looking back on her own life, she sees many kinds of roots intertwining and working to make her life what it is. She mentions early home experiences, decades of marriage to a husband she can pray with about important issues, years of attendance at church, and wide reading of books that contain the stories of others' lives. Like many of our saints, she is conscious of the ways in which people have loved, taught, and prayed for her, and of how the way her life has unfolded is something of a gift.

Ultimately, says writer Kenneth Woodward, "only God can make saints."[2] The saints we have met thus far confirm that sanctity is not a technique to be mastered, nor is it a mere matter of willpower. They speak too often of others' help and God's serendipitous leadings to allow us to think that sainthood is something superficially transmitted or casually replicated.

Nor are the lives of the saints just models for us woodenly to imitate. This is true not only of the saints among us, but also of those whom the church has historically identified as worthy of emulation. The lives of the classic, historic saints, says historian Robert Wilken, "arouse, judge, inspire, challenge, surprise, amuse, disturb, and excite the reader. . . . [Their lives], in Karl Jasper's words, serve more as 'beacons by which to gain an orientation' than as 'models to imitate.' Not everyone can or will pursue the same path."[3]

Yet there are things we can learn from the saints among us—things that help us understand how they got to be the way they are and that suggest paths for our own creative sanctity. As we explored in our interviews the turns and detours of their lives, we found signposts that can orient and guide our fledgling saintliness. We discovered that the saints, for all their varied lifestyles and backgrounds, are likely to have certain experiences and moments of discovery in common. Understanding these can point us to a new road of growth and progress toward a more saintly life.

First, many of the saints find their character honed by humble circumstances and simple life beginnings. For all the influence they have on society, they are certainly not confined to the cultural centers that host the country's think tanks and prestigious educational institutions. Sheila Solomon, a saint whose comments appear several times throughout this book, lives in a small Georgia town that is surrounded by farm fields of corn, tobacco, and peanuts. "It's at least sixty miles to a town with a good shopping center," she observes. A number of saints live in towns, while others are found on farms, and a number in urban areas and suburbs. Some of our saints wrote answers in the tortured English of someone whose schooling has been minimal. While many were quite articulate, others revealed a simplicity of speech and expression that suggested little formal education.

The data confirm that the circumstances of the humble and unsophisticated not only do not discourage sainthood, they may actually encourage it. The proportion of saints among us rises steadily as education levels decrease. Consider these numbers: among college graduates, roughly 10 percent meet our criteria for sainthood. Among those who have an incomplete college education or a technical school background, the percentage is closer to 11. Among those with only high school education, the figure rises to 14. For those with less than high school, it is more than 17, and among those with only grade school education, the percentage is over 21.

Income figures reveal similar patterns favoring society's non-elite. As income rises, saintliness as we have defined it decreases. Those earning at least $40,000 a year have 10 percent of their number in the saint category. Among those earning $25,000 to $40,000, the number rises slightly to 10.2. Thirteen percent of those earning $15,000 to $25,000 are saints, and those who earn less than $15,000 yield a substantial 19 percent. Put more simply, 10 percent of those making $25,000 are saints among us, compared with over 16 percent of those in the under-$25,000 group. Wealth seems to be an obstacle to saintliness, a finding that echoes the teachings of many of history's great religious figures.

If one also considers that a higher proportion of saints is found among Southerners, among nonwhites (22 percent compared to 11; the figure for blacks only is 25 percent), and among women (15 versus 11 percent), a startling portrait emerges. A poor, black, Southern woman is more likely to be a saint among us than an American not sharing those characteristics. As we have noted, this "typical saint" does not fit society's stereotype of the influential citizen.

What does this tell us? Clearly, economic hardship, region, and skin color do not guarantee sanctity. Merely reducing someone's salary will not make them a saint. Ignorance and lack of education come with their own perils and limitations. So there are limits to the theological significance we can ascribe to this fascinating finding. And a host of sociological reasons may explain why poor, less educated nonwhites are more likely than others to meet our criteria for sainthood.

But we also suspect that the humble saint's experiences and circumstances may do more to build character and faith than the life of the average middle-class suburbanite. In the midst of the explosion of information in every field of knowledge the better educated among us may have missed something. Our society is saturated with knowledge but starving for wisdom. Our method of educating the young has more or less succeeded in imparting data but not necessarily in instilling character. Advertisers and the entertainment media have fed our hunger to "get ahead" and make more to spend more. But many of our country's less well off and many who come up with the short end of the educational stick have learned something more profound about what truly matters. As Paul told his first-century congregation at Corinth, not many of our saints were "wise by human standards; not many were influential; not many were of noble birth." Still, Paul concluded, "God chose the foolish things of this world to shame the wise; God chose the weak things of this world to shame the strong" (1 Cor. 1:27, NIV). "Blessed are the poor in spirit," Jesus said, "for theirs is the kingdom of heaven" (Matt. 5:3, NIV). Through the difficulty of their lives many of the saints among us dramatically learned lessons about dependence on God, the dignity and value of all human beings, and finding meaning and joy even in simple circumstance and everyday life.

This profile of the saints among us suggests that spiritual growth and character development have little to do with the trappings of economic and institutional success. The saints remind us that wisdom is found in unlikely places, not just in the big, extravagant, and showy things of society. They have found richness and wisdom even in the midst of social stigma, economic disadvantage, and personal reversals.

Our task, if we wish to grow toward sainthood, is to pay attention to the lessons we can learn from the disappointments of our lives. We need to be open to the kind of insights that are not limited to those of the corporate boardroom, college classroom, or slick advertisement. And we may find that simplifying our schedules and our spending habits gives us space for more richness in life, not less.

A cover story on a simple life "revolution in progress" in *Time* magazine suggests that Americans may be ripe for such insights. "In place of materialism," the story declared, "many Americans are embracing simpler pleasures and homier values. They've been thinking hard about what really matters in their lives, and they've decided to make some changes. What matters is having time for family and friends, rest and recreation, good deeds and spirituality. . . . The pursuit of a simpler life with deeper meaning is a major shift in America's private agenda."[4]

The saints can encourage us to a kind of simplicity that is more than a trend, but a genuine part of our faith and life.

Second, the saints remind us that Christian growth is not a do-it-yourself project. Here we have not so much statistical data as the collected insights taken from our interviews. We found that time after time people were decisive in the saints' growth in faith and life. God speaks through a "still, small voice" and sometimes guides a person directly through the Holy Spirit. Yet many respondents credited everyday people with who they are and what they had become. When we asked, "Who or what has had the most important influence on your religious faith?" almost all mentioned a person: a parent, spouse, neighbor, Sunday school teacher, pastor, even their own children.

Sometimes these shaping relationships were not elaborate or set in the context of a religious institution. One man we interviewed spoke of his grandfather being instrumental in his faith development. "He was old, retired, blind. I would go to his house to talk with him, and would sit on his knee." Not only the talks they had, but also the grandfather's presence and availability left a great impression.

One saint among us told of how hearing her pastor's sermons, and spending informal time with his wife made her faith become more genuine and life-changing. "I got close to them," she says, "when I was pregnant and staying at home. His wife and I worked on the church newsletter together. Sometimes we went shopping together." Both the sermons she heard from the pastor and the informal modeling and friendship she experienced with his wife led her to a new level of spiritual commitment.

Another told a poignant story of learning through the

compassion of another that God cared for her. "I was the oldest child in the family. My dad rejected me because I wasn't a boy. I never felt worthy. But a pastor helped me see that I was worthy, that God cared for me as my father never did. Somebody finally cared for me the way I was, right then and there. Through my pastor's words and caring, and through the Bible, I learned of God's love."

Whether it was a father who ensured that the family "said grace" before meals, an adult child who returned home from college with a revitalized faith, a Sunday school teacher who showed great interest in students, or a neighbor who took time to talk about how faith had made a difference, a cast of people emerged as essential in explaining the lives of the saints among us. Says Episcopal pastor and writer Alan Jones, "God has so ordained things that we grow in the Spirit only through the frail instrumentality of one another."[5] Fourth-century church leader Augustine put it simply: "No one can walk without a guide." The saints remind us that growth requires others who listen, encourage, model, and instruct. To grow in sanctity, all of us need mentors, guides, and teachers whose influence lives on inside us in large and sometimes hidden ways.

Third, the saints remind us to live a life open to a transcendent God. "The saint is not a saint because he is good," theologian Paul Tillich is supposed to have once said, "but because he is transparent for something that is larger than he is." In their different ways, the saints all talked of God as one who was more than just a pleasant thought or benign deity, but one who through his greatness had the power to make their lives different. Of course, they all answered "agree" or "strongly agree" to the question, "God gives me strength, that I would not otherwise have, to forgive people who have hurt me deeply." In the follow-up contacts the saints mentioned a wide range of other ways a transcendent God had made a discernible difference in their lives. One told of answered prayer. "Our adult son lost his job and had to come back home to live with us. I prayed every night for him before I went to bed. Jobs were scarce. But I felt God saying, 'I'm going to help you and your son.' And he did."

A middle-aged man from the Midwest recounted an incident where he had been talking about his religious faith to a friend who didn't believe in God. "When my friend was asking questions, I had more knowledge than I thought I had. I really didn't know where it all came from. The Holy Spirit was with me."

Still another saint among us, Nancy Longhurst, began believing in God in the first place through a dawning awareness of transcendence. "I was taking a science class in college. Everything in the world seemed so complex and perfectly engineered. I just couldn't believe it happened from a 'Big Bang.' I got to thinking that the world must have been created. I asked my sister to take me to a church where the teachings of Christianity would be clearly presented. I was baptized and joined that summer."

In all their varied experiences of God's transcendence, the saints we talked with would probably agree with the saint who said, "I can't understand how people who have no faith can make it through life." God is too much of a helper and powerful presence in their lives to think that their lives would be the same without this dimension of transcendence.

This does not mean that faith is always a matter of absolute certainty for the saints. They experience the doubts that make up part of what it means to be human. When you are a believer, one of our saints observed, "you don't understand everything. You don't know what's going to happen. What happens when you die? Where does the body go? When does God take you to heaven?" One saint confessed, "Sometimes I scream at God." But normal doubts and struggles aside, the saints do seem to live with a conviction that inevitably affects the ways they go about their lives.

British church leader John Stott once spoke of this dimension. "When we meet some people we know immediately and instinctively that they are different. We are anxious to learn their secret. [The secret is not found in] the way they dress or talk or behave, although it influences these things. It is not that they have affixed a name tag to themselves and proclaimed themselves the adherent of a particular religion or ideology. It's not even that they have a strict moral code which they faithfully follow. It is that they know Jesus Christ, and that he is a living reality to them. They dwell in him and he dwells in them. He is the source of their life and it show in everything they do."[6]

In a day when pop psychology and New Age philosophies tell us that we should make our own self the center of our lives, the saints remind us that only by opening ourselves to the transcendent do we become the people we were made to be. A recent article in *Time* magazine, commenting on the materialism and consumerism that still attracts many baby boomers, quotes an advertising executive who says, "There is a free-floating sense of searching for a value system. All the instincts of the baby boomers are saying, 'Slow down. Figure out what's important.' But they haven't arrived at what that is."[7] The saints among us have found "what it is" and can lead a generation of people in search of something bigger than themselves to a more enduring truth.

Finally, the saints remind us that life is meant to be lived for others before it is lived for ourselves. We become saintly when we break out of self-absorption or the stresses of everyday living long enough think about the needs of others. There is great value in "knowing oneself," of course. "The unexamined life is not worth living," Socrates is to have said. But our day has perhaps taken introspection to ultimately destructive lengths. While the addiction recovery movement, for example, has helped many find healing and a deeper sense of who they are, has it also become an addiction itself? Are thousands struggling to find evidence of dysfunction and abuse in their childhood to the extent that concern for others is squeezed out?[8]

The saints among us, we found, manifest a healthy willingness to help others. Almost three quarters of them claim in survey questions to spend a great deal of time helping people in need, and the saints we interviewed could all point to ways, simple or large, in which they invested themselves in others.

It may be no accident that Jesus' parable of the Good Samaritan, with its emphasis on caring for others, stands out as perhaps his best-known teaching. Something in us resonates with the story of selfless giving. The saints among us show us that sainthood involves such thinking of others, even if only sometimes in small ways. The family members we live with, the neighbors we greet in our apartment complex hallway, the bosses we work for, or the homeless strangers we pass on busy streets all provide us with moments wherein we can share ourselves. The saints seize these opportunities more than most of us. They seem to model the verse in the New Testament that says, "Anyone who does not love his brother, whom he has seen, cannot love God, whom he has not seen" (1 John 4:20, NIV).

In the midst of all these insights about becoming more saintly, there is a recurrent tension. Christianity has always understood saintliness to involve grace—God's enabling, empowering presence, which all our saints would acknowledge as essential in one way or another. But if sanctity and goodness are gifts, they are also qualities we cultivate. The elements of sainthood we have discussed above require of us a decision and intentional participation. Becoming a saint means both openness and effort, waiting and action. "Just as human relationships mature through the years when carefully cultivated," writes educator Iris Cully, "so the relationship to God, which we call the spiritual life, can only be developed slowly." God is the teacher, she notes, and spiritual guides who are further along than us are assistants. The growth in spiritual maturity and saintliness is a lifelong enterprise.[9] Ways in which churches and church leaders can help in that process will form the focus of our last chapter.

8

Nurturing Would-be Saints

The development of piety lies in an openness to the work of the Holy Spirit. The cultivation of God's presence is renewed every day. The Spirit is like the wind, blowing everywhere, alternately still and gusty. The gentle breeze comforts; the gale cannot be contained. So humans, daring to call upon the Spirit, must be ready to accept whatever manifestations are given.

—Iris Cully[1]

An eighteenth-century Hebrew story tells of a young man who wanted to become a blacksmith. He became an apprentice and learned all the techniques of the trade: holding the tongs, smiting the anvil, working the bellows. When his training was done, he found a job at the palace smithy. But all his skill at using the tools turned out to be of no use: he had never learned to kindle a spark.[2]

Pastors, educators, parents, and others sometimes wonder if they are succeeding at "kindling the spark" of spiritual commitment and vitality. They wonder if the church is fulfilling its role in nurturing spiritual commitment and instilling values of compassion. Two nationwide surveys taken in 1988 place the questions in high relief. One showed that almost half of all Americans think the influence of religion is "decreasing."[3] The other showed that a majority of Americans (59 percent) strongly or moderately agree that "most churches and synagogues today are too concerned with organizational, as opposed to theological or spiritual issues."[4] Has the church's affair with institutional success turned spiritual nurture into a forgotten stepchild?

We believe that the saints have much to show the church and other value-shaping institutions. In our interviews we asked the saints among us questions about the influences that molded them. We looked at ways in which their faith had been formed and their compassion nourished. We sought to find out what parents, church leaders, and everyday citizens can learn for the task of nurturing and influencing others. While we do not claim to be experts in congregational management, developmental psychology, and spiritual formation, we have turned these discoveries into practical suggestions and long-term prescriptions for the church, for parents, and for any concerned with the spiritual vitality of society.

Starting with practical steps

We first offer these practical suggestions for nurturing sainthood in a secular world:

Provide opportunities for people to give of themselves in service. Tom Davies, whom we met earlier, reflects, "I'd like to do more to help others, but sometimes I don't see the opportunities. Sometimes our lifestyles are rather impersonal. It's not like it was when you'd live in a small village and you'd know the people who need help. I live in an apartment complex where I hardly know another person. There must be people out there—an old person who needs someone to visit, for example—but I don't know where they are. They aren't a part of my daily life." The church and other institutions of society need to consider ways to tap into this reserve of willingness by offering people avenues for the expression of such compassionate impulses. Seminary professor and writer George Hunter notes, "Because of factors like early retirement . . . we have more and more people in this country looking for something useful to do with their discretionary time—useful in the sense that if they did it, it would really make a difference. . . . Here you have a people with gifts and skills and energies, all dressed up with nowhere to go. To make worthwhile service an option for them and combine it with the opportunity to do something new would find a harvest, I believe."[5]

The need of churches and other groups to provide such opportunities may explain in part a finding by Robert Wuthnow, mentioned earlier, that "the more often a person claims to experience divine love, the more likely that person is to spend time on charitable activities. *But this effect is limited to individuals who attend church regularly*" (emphasis added).[6] Churches are vital in ensuring that society's current interest in spirituality moves beyond mere private piety. They can play a vital role in nurturing and providing practical expression for the religiously motivated desire to help others.

Encourage the development of small groups. One of our saints told a story of attending a small prayer meeting at a church. She recalls that the people in the group spoke of God giving people a "new name," a name that had to do with love and acceptance. It became for her a moment of great insight. "I was giving myself a 'shaming' name, but through their prayers I was able suddenly to hear God saying to me, 'That's not the way I see you. I want to give you an endearing name, not a shaming name. I see you in a loving way.'"

A recent Gallup survey reveals that four Americans in ten have participated in small support groups. Twenty-eight percent are involved in such groups that meet regularly and provide caring and support for their members. An additional 10 percent say they would like to become involved.[7] Eighty-five percent of these say the groups helped respondents "to serve people outside the group." Seventy-four percent say the groups helped them "feel closer to God."[8] Americans clearly see value in coming together with others for personal development and growth. The church and other religious institutions need to take full advantage of the benefits of such gatherings.

Encourage people to find spiritual mentors or prayer partners. One saint we talked with spoke of working at "watching people at church who are more mature than I am—and walking as they walk." Margie Dennie tells of one woman in particular who became a spiritual mentor for her when she was in high school. "She got me involved in a weekly Bible study. I saw how God had changed her life, had made a difference. I saw her personal relationship with Christ. Seeing her faith helped me. Being with her and with the others in the group, seeing their commitment, helped me to strengthen my own." Now that Margie is an adult, "I see myself in a similar role to others. I see God using me to touch the lives of others in the same way he used this woman's life to influence me."

One could argue that every person needs a spiritual counselor or a faith partner of some sort, a person with whom to share innermost spiritual feelings—a member of the clergy, a friend, a husband or wife, a parent, or a child.

Accent the spiritual reality of the Christian faith. As our stories have shown, and as studies confirm, many people, churched and unchurched, have had deep religious experiences. Too often these are dismissed, even by religious leaders, as autosuggestion or emotionalism. In one way or another, our saints consistently find prayer and religious experience crucial to their growth and self-understanding. They can point to specific ways in which God has transformed or is now transforming their lives.

One saint from Nashville tells this story: "I was told by doctors I needed surgery for a serious condition. At the same time my sister became very ill. I needed to take care of her. I prayed with my pastor about it. And I became able to take of my sister—for five years. Then she died, and only then did my condition return. I had to have the surgery, but I saw the timing of it all as a true answer to prayer."

Profound experiences like these can open wonderful opportunities for group discussion. Says seminary professor and writer George Hunter, "The problem we find in many churches is that people are experiencing the grace of God, and deep needs are being met. Good things are happening in their lives that nobody hears about. In most churches we do not have the structural opportunities set up to encourage people to talk about what God is doing in their lives, or what they want God to do in their lives. That means that a church can have remarkable things happening in it and most of the people don't hear about it."[9]

Provide opportunities (and training) for evangelism and other means of reaching those not involved. A good thing is worth sharing with others. A number of our saints are concerned about—and, as John Fafinski's story showed, successful at—sharing their faith with others. Many, however, need encouragement and guidance. "It's hard knowing how to be a loving witness in the place where I work," said one of our saints. "The atmosphere is hostile to Christian things. I try to pray for individuals in the office. I hope the way I am shows them that since becoming a Christian I'm slightly different. A couple of times I've been able to share my faith verbally. But it's an area I need to grow in."

The value of helping the saints to help others find faith and become involved in church is underlined in the "Unchurched American" Gallup survey of 1988. It showed not only high levels of traditional religious belief among the unchurched, but also indicated that 58 percent of the unchurched would "definitely," "probably," or "possibly" return to church sometime in the future. Many on the fringe or outside of faith communities simply await an invitation from a friend or acquaintance to join.[10]

Longer-term strategies

Beyond these more practical suggestions, we also offer the following long-term strategies for leaders and parents wanting to help saints in the making:

First, the work of nurturing saints needs to begin with the young. Our interviews confirmed that we should not wait until the so-called "age of accountability" to help children in our care to understand God and the importance of living for others. The unusual commitment of the saints was in many cases traceable to experiences and relationships from earliest childhood. A number of our saints could remember special Sunday school teachers, neighbors, relatives, and, of course, parents who made a world of difference in their formation.

One saint described this vital role of an early Sunday school superintendent and teacher: "My mother passed away when I was seven. I never really knew her. But this woman was like a mother to me—to everyone, really. Children would go to church just to hear her tell stories from the Bible. I could always go to her if I needed advice, if I needed someone to talk to." It is undoubtedly no accident that our saint in turn became a Sunday school teacher when she reached adulthood.

The concern for nurture begins at the earliest moments

of life, education theorists argue. Says educator Iris Cully, even infants—who are too young to understand words such as "God" or "grace"—need a nurturing and loving environment that will help them develop the capacity to trust, and thereby build a capacity for being able later to believe in and trust God.[11] And "as soon as a child begins to understand words," she says, "believing parents will frequently spend a moment at bedtime referring joyfully to the spent day's events, speaking of God, and in a connecting gesture softly touching the child's hands or head."[12]

This kind of early nurture and positive association with the things of faith will not guarantee saintliness, of course, but it can ready the soil for the flowering of a later commitment. Sociologist Robert Wuthnow tells of one man he interviewed who reflected, "If you grow up going to Sunday school and hearing about the Good Samaritan and the miracles of Jesus and the beatitudes, you can't help having some of it rub off on you."[13] He was perhaps a bit optimistic, especially considering that 82 percent of Americans claim to have had religious training in childhood—far more than ended up as saints among us.[14] Nevertheless, seeds sown among even the very young may some day take root and grow.

Parish pastor David Stokes writes, "When a child is grown, when he or she is hedged about with difficulties and uncertainties, after the childish enthusiasms have faded and the emotionalism of adolescence no longer delivers, it is usually that one strange individual from long ago with a quiet but passionate love of the Faith who functions as an anchor. We may not know where they are, nor remember precisely what they said. But his or her character remains etched in our psyches, a fixed point of reference by which we try to determine what God would have us to be."[15]

Second, nurturing sainthood is a process that builds on developmental "windows" and unexpected moments of teachability. Paul the apostle spoke of faith as a maturing process whereby believers grow from spiritual infancy into maturity (Eph. 4:13), from the ability to take only spiritual "milk" to the capacity to have "solid food" (1 Cor. 3:2, NIV).

For many of our saints faith was preeminently a process, a series of turning points when truth became real in fresh ways or commitment took on new depth. Dotty Biros's story in the first chapter illustrates this journey-like quality of faith; hers is a story of faith moving from less mature expressions in childhood and early adulthood to become a new creative, healing force in middle age. This confirms what Christian educators have known all along: developmental "stages" present a series of varied opportunities to nurture faith and spiritual commitment.

The age when children begin school, for example, is a time of acquiring new skills and independence. This usually also entails a healthy curiosity about how the world came to be, who God is, and what it means to relate considerately to others. Adults need to be alert and ready not only to model, but also to articulate the beliefs and values that comprise their faith.

Adolescence, with its sometimes tumultuous changes, presents other special problems and opportunities in nurturing saints. For many the teenage years represent a time of profound searching and powerful peer pressures. Margie Dennie, whom we met in chapter 2, tells of how a small Bible study group made all the difference for her in high school. "Being in a group of people who knew me, prayed for me, and wanted to see me succeed helped give me a 'keeping power' when I faced temptations, when I faced times when I could go either way. Knowing that I would affect people who had invested in me helped me stay on the right track."

If adolescence is, as some developmental theorists believe, best characterized by a search for identity, it is then more than ever that they need role models. Teens apparently think often about faith matters; a recent survey shows that the great majority of teens believe God loves them (93 percent). Three in ten report having experienced the presence of God in some way.[16] An earlier Gallup survey found that nearly half of older teens have had a "crisis of faith."[17] In the light of such ferment, public school teachers, pastors, and church leaders need to ensure that saints are part of the circle of influence in a teen's life. Small groups, Sunday school classes, and other avenues of Christian nurture are important not just for the beliefs that are articulated, but for the modeling that happens, the spontaneous interaction that helps faith be "caught" as well as taught.

Such nurture also has relevance for college-age youth, especially now, when fewer students are educated at church-related colleges and instead attend schools where tax assistance arrives with the expectation that there will be no classroom discussions of morality, ethics, religion, even meaning and purpose. This creates a significant vacuum in the lives of many young people at the very time they are making key decisions about vocation, religious affiliation, and marriage.

Third, nurturing sainthood means recognizing that spiritual education and development does not end at the threshold of adulthood. Many of our saints had profoundly deepening experiences as adults. A number of our saints, such as the colleague of John Fafinski quoted in chapter 5, became believers as adults. One 74-year-old saint we interviewed summed up her approach to

God and life over the decades as "keeping an open heart and mind." But sometimes adults see themselves as having developed spiritually all they ever will. Spirituality is not seen as the province of adult concerns. William O'Malley, who teaches theology and English at an East Coast prep school reflects, "I wonder . . . whether just as most Christians left learning about God (theology) back in high school or college, they also left learning to know God better (spirituality) back in grad school or on their mother's lap, if they learned it there."[18]

One life-cycle window of opportunity of special relevance for our time concerns the so-called "baby boomers" and their much-publicized return to religion in recent years. According to the December 17, 1990 issue of *Newsweek*, many who left the church years ago have returned. It reports that "at one time or another, roughly two thirds of baby boomers dropped out of organized religion. But in recent years, more than one third of the dropouts have returned. About 57 percent—43 million people—now attend church or synagogue."[19] The church needs to be ready when such people come back searching for spiritual reality.

One of the reasons for the baby boomers' return, interestingly, concerns the advent of parenthood and the realization that their children need to learn solid values and "make friends with peers who share them."[20] More than one of our saints mentioned their children as instrumental in the deepening of faith. One saint from New Mexico, when asked who was influential in her faith development, wrote, "My children! They have been my strength and more often than not the catalyst to stay serving God even when I felt I wanted to give up, when I had times I felt weak and didn't want to serve God. I'd think about my kids and what would happen to them. It was a moral support."

Ray Pool of Canoga Park, California notes that when his daughter became involved in a Campus Crusade for Christ fellowship in college, she would come home and spark "heated discussions" about theological issues. "And she won," Ray says. "Next to my mother, my daughter was one of the most influential people in my spiritual growth. I had served as deacon and elder at the church I attended at the time, but these were not real spiritual experiences. After our discussions at home, I started going to another, more evangelical church. Things started happening."

Church leaders need to note that spirituality in the middle and later years may have a more sober, less dependent quality to it than that of adolescence. Men and women face anew issues of identity, career goals, financial security, mortality, and marriage stability. The resources of church and faithful Christians can be vital in helping them negotiate the hopes and pains of daily life.

Fourth, nurturing sainthood is a prime task of parenting. From the early days of the people of Israel as recorded in the Old Testament, people of faith have been enjoined to teach God's words of instruction "to your children, talking about them when you sit at home and when you walk along the road, when you lie down and when you get up" (Deut. 11:19, NIV). In the New Testament, Paul urged parents to bring up their children in the "training and instruction of the Lord" (Eph. 6:4, NIV).

Not surprisingly, then, a number of our saints mentioned mothers and fathers as crucial in their religious development. In many cases, both parents were influential, as in the case of one Kentucky saint who recalled this picture for us: "My parents were church-going people. All I knew was that Sunday was for church. We always said a blessing at the table." But several of saints that responded to our mail questionnaire indicated that their fathers had

had little or no influence in their growth in the faith. One saint even suggested that "the life pattern he had should have made me go against God." While our sample size for the follow-up interviews keeps us from drawing firm conclusions, such responses suggest that fathers may have had a smaller role than mothers in the formation of the saints among us. Churches and religious leaders should consider ways to support and deepen the faith of its fathers so that both parents can provide spiritual leadership in the home.

But this support should not be limited to men. A recent Gallup survey suggests that the religious influence of the home in general may be waning. Whereas 41 percent of respondents in a 1978 survey said they had received their religious training at home, only 28 percent responded this way in 1988, a thirteen-point drop.[21] Those wanting to nurture would-be saints need to be sure to include the home. Christian education professor Donald Joy notes, "Fathers and mothers, just in the business of doing their parenting, are unwittingly the [child's] first curriculum for representing God."[22]

Fifth, nurturing sainthood requires the corporate resources of the church. The saints among us give the lie to the idea that spirituality is a solitary exercise. "The individual is strengthened by the presence of other believers," says Iris Cully. "One is taught scripture by listening to readings from the Bible; one learns how to pray by participating in the prayer of the people of God."[23]

Much happens to shape a heart in the simple practice of regular worship with a congregation of fellow believers. Sunday school, small groups, youth groups, and other church functions outside of worship were all mentioned by our saints as having a role to play in their growing faith. Also, service projects can help instill in children from an early age the habit of helping.

The corporate dimension of nurturing will be enhanced as well by the telling of stories. Hearing people tell of convictions, struggles, triumphs, and values can leave great impressions. "The best way to rediscover God's involvement with us is through the telling of our stories—our testimonies," writes Mennonite pastor Arthur Paul Boers. "[But] sharing should not be limited to predictable formulas where everyone lives happily ever after once they have been converted," he cautions. "We should not hear only dramatic tales of conversion or the overcoming of impossible obstacles. Small struggles often speak most deeply." He tells of a congregation that has a monthly series called "People on the Way," that gives church members a chance to share what God is doing in their lives in the here and now.[24] Opportunities to hear what others have learned are too infrequent in the church.

Finally, nurturing sainthood is preeminently the work of the Spirit. We cannot exhaust all the elements that help commitment germinate. Not only is the matter complex, but there is also an element of God's gracious unpredictability that defies reduction to steps or formulas. "The wind blows wherever it pleases," Jesus once said. "You hear its sound, but you cannot tell where it comes from or where it is going. So it is with everyone born of the Spirit" (John 3:8, NIV).

Speaking of the classic saints of church history, historian Robert Wilken notes that whatever their varied lives and patterns, "the point in common is that the saint, like a plant that bends and twists to receive the sun, follows the course of God, always turning to the light that is the source of life."[25] That is an apt description of the ultimate reality at the heart of the saints' lives we have profiled in this book. Perhaps nothing better explains them than the God they turn to and claim to experience in their day-to-day lives.

Appendices

A

Saints Among Us Self-Test and Survey Sample

The following is the twelve-question survey we used in finding the saints among us.

	Strongly Agree 1	2	3	Strongly Disagree 4	5	Don't Know 0
a. My religious faith is the most important influence in my life.	1	2	3	4	5	0
b. I seek God's will through prayer.	1	2	3	4	5	0
c. I believe that God loves me even though I may not always obey him.	1	2	3	4	5	0
d. I try hard to put my religious beliefs into practice in my relations with all people, regardless of their backgrounds.	1	2	3	4	5	0
e. I receive comfort and support from my religious beliefs.	1	2	3	4	5	0
f. I believe that Jesus Christ was fully human and fully divine.	1	2	3	4	5	0
g. I wish my religious beliefs were stronger.	1	2	3	4	5	0
h. I believe in the full authority of the Bible.	1	2	3	4	5	0
i. I do things I don't want to do because I believe it is the will of God.	1	2	3	4	5	0
j. God gives me the strength, that I would not otherwise have, to forgive people who have hurt me deeply.	1	2	3	4	5	0
k. I try to bring others to Christ through the way I live or through discussion or prayer.	1	2	3	4	5	0
l. I wish my relationships with other Christians were stronger.	1	2	3	4	5	0

If you answered 1 or 2 (strongly agree or agree) to all twelve questions, you fit the criteria of "sainthood" detailed in this book.

B

For Further Reflection

Introduction

1. How would you answer the question posed by a friend of one of the authors: "Who are your heroes?"
2. A survey by researchers James Patterson and Peter Kim cited in the Introduction indicated that 70 percent of Americans polled say that we have no living heroes and that our children have no meaningful role models. Do you agree? How would you defend your position against someone who disagrees with you?
3. Do you think that trying to put "calipers" on (i.e., apply measuring instruments to) faith and commitment, such as we have done in our research into saints among us, is fraught with potential problems?
4. How do you view the finding that 13 percent of our respondents (and therefore of Americans) are "saints"? Do you see it as encouraging that there are that many? Or are you disappointed that the number is not larger?
5. "For a society tempted to think that only a highly visible few—the Billy Grahams and Mother Teresas—make a difference, our research shows otherwise." Do you ever find yourself wondering if you can ever make a dent in the problems around you?

Chapter 1

1. What quality in Dotty Biros stands out most strongly for you? Does she remind you of anyone you know? If so, in what ways?

2. In what ways does "Sheilaism"—"just my own little voice"—fit the mood of our times? In what ways is it a superficial basis for faith and religious commitment?
3. Do you agree with the assertion that there appears to be a great deal of "extrinsic" religion around us that makes little difference in people's lives?
4. What images or reactions does the word "saint" elicit in you? How does Paul seem to use the terms in Ephesians 1:1 and Philippians 1:1? Look up the word in a concordance to see the various ways in which the Bible uses the term. How do some of those uses correspond to our definition of a saint as someone who is spiritually committed and personally compassionate?
5. Take the "self-test" in Appendix A, to understand the questions we used to find the saints and to see how you "scored." Were there any surprises?
6. A number of our saints, such as the retired nurse in Nashville, spoke of doing something because they "believed it was in accordance with God's will." Can you name something you did only because you believed God wanted it done?
7. Robert Wilken argues that "without examples, without imitation, there can be no human life or culture . . . no virtue or holiness." Do you agree? Is it usually true that "before we can become doers we must become spectators"?
8. Does Martin Luther's statement that "God rides the lame horse and carves the rotten wood" mean anything to you personally? Do you find it encouraging that God uses us even when we are imperfect?

Chapter 2

1. What are your preconceptions about saints and sainthood? Were you surprised by the great diversity and variety manifested by the saints among us?

2. Our profile of the saints will surprise some people. That saintliness and influence upon others seems greater among the poor and less educated is a striking discovery. What reasons can you find to explain this?
3. How would you answer the survey question, “Have you ever had a religous experience—that is, a particularly powerful religious insight or awakening?” Do you think saints like Margie Dennie have something to show us about the importance of being open to divine encounters?
4. What kinds of commitments have you made to God? Did Margie’s prayer, “I just want to be your servant,” strike you as a genuinely significant turning point? Have you made similar prayers? If so, when, and under what circumstances? If not, do you see yourself making such a prayer in the near future? What are some of the things that might hold you back from doing so?
5. Can you recall deeds of kindness you have performed recently? Do you think acts of charity are sufficient to change society, or do you think they also need to be complemented by social reform and large-scale institutional change? Giving food to a food pantry, for example, feeds people in the short term, but many argue that it does not change fundamental social problems. Do you think some people are called to one kind of helping (acts of charity, for instance) while others are called to working for societal reform?
6. Why do you think deep faith changes the way a person views people from different backgrounds or races? Read Galatians 3:28 and think about what it means in this context.
7. “Joy is the echo of God’s life within us,” said one writer. Do you agree? Do you know people who fit the stereotype of the deeply religious person as one who is dour and glum?
8. We say that the saints are often found among the lowly—“they give the lie to the assumption that only the well-placed and powerful can make a difference.” Do you find that personally encouraging?

Chapter 3

1. What reactions do you have to Allen Danforth's remarkable story?

2. Historian of American religion Martin Marty calls our society's recent interest in spirituality an "event of our era." Do you see signs of the burgeoning interest? What needs for intimacy and relationship with God do you think so-called New Age philosophies and spiritualities tap into? In what ways are such answers to people's religious longings counterfeit?

3. What are the dangers in the new emphasis on some circles on religious "experience"? What are the strengths and possibilities?

4. Do you agree that deep faith involves both mountaintop and everyday experiences? In what ways is it important to remain faithful even when we do not experience a miracle or see "handwriting on the wall"?

5. The saints, we said, "integrate work with worship, practicalities with prayer." In what ways do you attempt, like Brother Lawrence, to "practice the presence of God" in your daily round of duties and work?

6. This chapter recounts several ways in which the saints pray. In what different ways do you pray?

7. Do you agree with educator Iris Cully that spiritual growth "includes a conscious effort to develop"? What does that mean in your life? In what ways would you like to be more deliberate in your spiritual growth?

8. Jesus said, "Where two or three are gathered in my name, there am I with them." What does this say about the important corporate dimension of prayer and the spiritual life?

9. Do you agree that spiritual awareness at its best leads people to more concern about the hurts and hungers of the world?

How can we guard against prayer becoming a private, self-centered practice?

Chapter 4

1. At the time of Allen Danforth's "call" to raise money for relief, he could not have forseen the eventually dramatic results. How important was it for Allen to take a small step of obedience by saying yes to God when he was on the plane home from Honduras?
2. Review the statistics on the relationship between the saints' spiritual commitment and the likelihood of their saying that they spend "a good deal of time" helping those in need. How do you account for the seeming connection between faith and works, between religious commitment and social compassion?
3. Read James 2:17, 1 John 4:11, and Ephesians 5:1. What insights do these passages yield on the relationship between faith and love?
4. Of the saints' different motivations for helping others, which do you identify with most closely?
5. Does your personal experience confirm the Independent Sector/Gallup survey finding that regular churchgoers are "far more likely to give a higher percentage of their household income to charitable causes"?
6. To what extent are the problems of society "systemic," as sociologist Robert Wuthnow argues, and thereby in need of more than individual acts of charity?
7. What does Elton Trueblood mean when he suggests that ours is a "cut-flower civilization"? What does Nancy Longhurst's story have to do with the common good of society?
8. Glenn Tinder argues that we wrongly assume that we can

continue to treasure "the life and welfare, the civil rights and political authority, of every person without believing in a God who renders such attitudes and conduct compelling." Is he right? Why or why not?

Chapter 5

1. In what ways was John Fafinski successful in having an impact on people in his workplace? In terms of his sharing his faith, what part did his behavior play? His spoken witness? How important is it that a person's way of relating to others corroborates what he or she may say about God's love?
2. How does the New Testament character Dorcas (Acts 9:39) model the impact our lives can have through "small" acts? Do we sometimes forget how the little things we do count for something?
3. What is the relationship between faith and forgiveness? Why do you think spiritual people are more able to forgive than the general population? Reflect back on times when prayer made a difference, or could have, in the wake of your being wronged. Note the story of Jim Volovlek and how a worship service was the setting for a significant reconciliation.
4. What does Jesus mean in the Lord's Prayer when he teaches us to pray, "forgive us our trespasses, as we forgive those who trespass against us"? Look up Colossians 3:13. What does it say about forgiveness?
5. Call to mind someone you know or knew who was humble in a memorable way. How did this person make you feel? How is humility a virtue that makes room for others to talk or share of themselves?
6. Read Philippians 2:1–11. What does this tell us about Christ? What relevance does that have for understanding how we are to relate to others?

Chapter 6

1. Through a variety of studies we have shown a substantial connection between spiritual commitment and the tendency for one to see his or her life as satisfying and happy. In what ways do your own life and the lives of people close to you bear that out? Do you know any circumstances or people that seem to contradict that finding? In what ways?
2. Why do you think deeply religious people are often portrayed in entertainment media as overly pious and as gloomy?
3. Keith Miller talks about an experience of profound commitment that brought "a cessation of the conflict of a lifetime." How does a relationship with God help us move with peace through the times of turmoil in our lives? How does it stir up new issues, such as it did with Tom Davies?
4. Do you agree with Blaise Pascal that the closer one comes to God, "the happier one is, and the further away one goes, the more unhappy one is"?
5. A number of saints have found God's care to be tremendously significant during times of crisis. Have you found it so? When God does not lift us out of a difficult situation, can he be counted on to be a companion and friend? What does Romans 8:28 mean in this context?
6. How does faith help you to be less anxious or more hopeful when you look to the future?
7. Some observers note a new and growing awareness of personal mortality in our society. Does belief in God offer resources for those who face illness and death? How might convictions about an afterlife change our view of our own deaths?
8. Reread the paragraph that details writer Philip Yancey's observations about "stars" and "servants." While celebrities would appear, at least on the surface, to have many ingredi-

ents of a worry-free life, is that really the case? Does success, as many in society understand it, not ultimately satisfy our longings for meaning and love?

Chapter 7

1. None of the people we have profiled in this book are celebrities or in what are normally considered high-profile positions. Yet, through their spiritual commitment and compassionate orientations, they seem to be making a difference in others' lives. What does this suggest about the influence your own life may have or could have?
2. Are you surprised that the level of saintliness as we have defined it increases as educational level decreases? What does this say about the potential for making the most of humble circumstances? Is there something about being in society's less elite that is more conducive to sainthood?
3. Do you agree that "the humble saint's experiences and circumstances may do more to build character and faith than the life of the average middle class suburbanite"?
4. Read 1 Corinthians 1:26–27. What is Paul saying about the trappings of prestige? What do these verses suggest may be the transformed, "upside-down" values of the kingdom of God?
5. Do you agree with the *Time* magazine article that says that Americans are in "pursuit of a simpler life with deeper meaning"?
6. Alan Jones says, "God has so ordained things, that we grow in the Spirit only through the frail instrumentality of one another." How true has that been for you? Who are the people who have helped you grow? In what ways did they help?
7. The saints have a strong sense of the transcendence of God. This does not mean that they are perfected in their faith, however. "Sometimes I scream at God," one saint confessed.

What is the place of religious doubt and struggle and even anger with God?

8. The saints among us manifest a healthy willingness to live for others. In what ways is that a challenge to us who live in a society that encourages "looking out for number one"?

9. "Becoming a saint means both openness and effort, waiting and action." When these pairs of approaches to the spiritual life are kept in tension, how do they complement one another?

Chapter 8

1. How do you interpret the finding that a majority of Americans (59 percent) strongly or moderately agree that "most churches and synagogues today are too concerned with organizational, as opposed to theological or spiritual issues"? In what ways has your congregation balanced concern for institutional health (budgeting, administration, programming, staffing, etc.) and emphasis on spiritual vitality (pastoral care, worship, outreach, Christian nurture, and so on)?

2. How does the congregation you are associated with provide opportunities for people interested in volunteering time to help others? Are there areas of opportunity or need going unaddressed? Should you have some part to play in initiating something?

3. Have you ever been involved in a small group, church related or otherwise? What do you think is the genius of small group meetings? What can the church (and would-be saints) learn from Alcoholics Anonymous and other recovery groups?

4. What are some limitations of the "rugged individualism" that is still a part of our cultural climate? How might a prayer partner or spiritual mentor help you in your Christian growth?

5. What are the greatest hindrances you face when you think about sharing your faith with someone who is not a Christian? What obstacles or hesitations do people in your church experience?

6. Review the list of six long-term strategies for nurturing sainthood. In what strategy area are you or your church strongest? Identify two strategies that need further attention in your parenting, church leadership, or other avenue of influencing others. What practical steps can you take to further the nurture of saints in the next two months?

Notes

Introduction

1. James Patterson and Peter Kim, *The Day America Told the Truth* (New York: Prentice Hall, 1991), 27.
2. John Silber, *Straight Shooting* (New York: Harper and Row, 1989), 37–62.
3. John Delaney, ed., *Saints Are Now* (Garden City, NY: Doubleday, 1981), 9.

Chapter 1

1. John Delaney, ed., *Saints Are Now*, 9.
2. Kenneth L. Woodward, *Making Saints* (New York: Simon and Schuster, 1990), 403.
3. *Religion in America 1990* (Princeton, NJ: Princeton Religion Research Center, n.d.), 21, 45.
4. Alfie Kohn, "Do Religious People Help More? Not So You'd Notice," *Psychology Today* (December 1989), 68.
5. Robert N. Bellah, et al., *Habits of the Heart* (New York: Harper and Row, 1985), 221.
6. Robert Wilken, "The Lives of the Saints and the Pursuit of Virtue," *First Things* (December 1990), 45.
7. Ibid., 51.
8. Woodward, *Making Saints*, 403.
9. Evelyn Underhill, *The Ways of the Spirit* (New York: Crossroad, 1990), p. 85.
10. *Hymnbook 1982* (Episcopal hymnal) (New York: The Church Hymnal Corporation, 1985), #293.

Chapter 2

1. Oswald Chambers, *The Best from All His Books*, ed. Harry Verploegh, (Nashville: Oliver Nelson/Thomas Nelson, 1987), 297.
2. Phil. 3:17, NIV
3. George Gallup, Jr., and Sarah Jones, *100 Questions and Answers: Religion in America* (Princeton, NJ: Princeton Religion Research Center, 1989), 36.
4. Princeton Religion Research Center, "Highly Religious Are Most Likely to Feel Close to Families," *Emerging Trends* (June 1989), 1.
5. Robert Wuthnow, *Acts of Compassion* (Princeton, NJ: Princeton University Press, 1991), 154.
6. Thomas Merton, *The Seven Storey Mountain* (New York: Harcourt Brace Jovanovich, 1948, 1976), 415.
7. *Religion in America 1982* (Princeton, NJ: Princeton Religion Research Center, 1982), 58.
8. C. S. Lewis, *Mere Christianity* (New York: Macmillan, 1943, 1945, 1952), 187–88.

Chapter 3

1. Albert Camus, *The Plague*, quoted in Margaret Pepper, comp. and ed., *The Harper Religious and Inspirational Quotation Companion* (New York: Harper and Row, 1989), 371.
2. Blaise Pascal, *Pensées*, quoted in Pepper, ibid., 370.
3. Martin Marty, *Context* (January 1, 1990), 1–2.
4. George Gallup, Jr., and Jim Castelli, *The People's Religion* (New York: Macmillan, 1989), 68.
5. Thomas Merton, *The Ascent to Truth* (San Diego: Harcourt Brace Jovanovich, 1951, 1979), 185.
6. Brother Lawrence, *The Practice of the Presence of God* (Old Tappan, NJ: Fleming H. Revell), 8.

7. Iris V. Cully, *Education for Spiritual Growth* (San Francisco: Harper and Row, 1984), 33.
8. Margaret M. Poloma and George H. Gallup, Jr., *Varieties of Prayer* (Philadelphia: Trinity Press, 1991), 25.
9. Ibid., 29–31.
10. Robert N. Bellah, Richard Madsen, William M. Sullivan, Ann Swidler, and Steven M. Tipton, *Habits of the Heart* (New York: Harper and Row, 1985), 84.
11. Fyodor Dostoyevsky, *The Brothers Karamazov* (New York: The Modern Library, 1950), 40.

Chapter 4

1. Bernard Shaw, *Man and Superman* (epistle dedicatory) in *Seven Plays* (New York: Dodd, and Mead, 1967), 510–11.
2. Wuthnow, *Acts of Compassion*, 51.
3. Ibid.
4. Ibid.
5. Gallup and Castelli, 231–32.
6. Ibid., 5.
7. Susan Champlin Taylor, "Talents, Tools and Time," *Modern Maturity* (April–May 1990), 79.
8. "For Goodness' Sake," *Time* (January 9, 1989), 21.
9. Princeton Religion Research Center, "Here Come the Baby Boomers," *Emerging Trends* (June 1991), 5.
10. Princeton Religion Research Center, "Voluntarism Runs Deep in U.S. Society," *Emerging Trends* (November 1989), 3.
11. "Religious Faith: Firm Foundation for Charity," *Christianity Today* (November 19, 1990), 63.
12. Wuthnow, *Acts of Compassion*, 6, 7.
13. "For Goodness Sake," 21.
14. "Idealism's Rebirth," *U.S, News & World Report* (October 24, 1988), 37–38.

15. Wuthnow, *Acts of Compassion*, 240.
16. Ibid., 239.
17. Thomas Merton, *No Man Is an Island* (New York: Harcourt Brace Jovanovich, 1955), 127.
18. Elton Trueblood, *The Predicament of Modern Man* (New York and London: Harper and Brothers, 1944), 59–60.
19. Glenn Tinder, "Can We Be Good Without God?" *The Atlantic Monthly* (December 1989), 76, 80, 82.

Chapter 5

1. Richard Foster, *Celebration of Discipline* rev. ed. (San Francisco: Harper and Row, 1988), 135.
2. Phyllis McGinley, *Saint-Watching* (New York: Viking, 1969), 18.
3. François Fénelon, *Christian Perfection* (Minneapolis: Bethany Fellowship, 1975), 34, quoted in Foster, *Celebration of Discipline*,136.
4. Poloma and Gallup, *Varieties of Prayer*, 85–106.
5. Ibid., 102.
6. Quoted in Foster, *Celebration of Discipline*, 131.
7. Evelyn Underhill, *The Spiritual Life*, quoted in Rueben P. Job and Norman Shawchuck, *A Guide to Prayer* (Nashville: Upper Room, 1983), 86.

Chapter 6

1. Quoted in Horton Davies, ed., *The Communion of Saints* (Grand Rapids, MI: William B. Eerdmans, 1990), 32.
2. William James, *The Varieties of Religious Experience* (New York: Modern Library, 1902, 1936), 274
3. *Religion in America 1982*, 52–53, 58.
4. Princeton Religion Research Center, *Emerging Trends* (June 1989), 1.

5. Wuthnow, *Acts of Compassion*, 291.
6. Keith Miller, *A Taste of New Wine* (Waco, TX: Word Books, 1965), 39.
7. Quoted in James Houston, *In Search of Happiness* (Batavia, IL: Lion, 1990), 137.
8. Ibid., 241–42.
9. James, *Varieties of Religious Experience*, 267.
10. Ibid., 284.
11. Quoted in Houston, *In Search of Happiness*, 237.
12. No author, *Religion in America 1990*, 25.
13. Michael Specter, "Hot Tombs," *The New Republic* (September 11, 1989), 22–23.
14. Philip Yancey, "Low Pay, Long Hours, No Applause," *Christianity Today* (November 18, 1988), 80.
15. Iris V. Cully, *Education for Spiritual Growth* (San Francisco: Harper & Row, 1984), 1.

Chapter 7

1. Quoted in Avery Brooke, *Finding God in the World* (San Francisco: Harper and Row, 1989), 49.
2. Woodward, *Making Saints*, 406.
3. Wilken, "The Lives of the Saints," 51.
4. Janice Castro, "The Simple Life," *Time* (April 8, 1991), 58.
5. Alan Jones, *Exploring Spiritual Direction* (New York: Seabury, 1982), 79.
6. Quoted in Princeton Religion Research Center, *Emerging Trends* (February, 1984).
7. Walter Shapiro, "The Birth and—Maybe—Death of Yuppies," *Time* (April 8, 1991), 65.
8. Gerald May, *The Awakened Heart*, (San Francisco: Harper San Francisco, 1991), 16.
9. Cully, *Education for Spiritual Growth*, 14.

Chapter 8

1. Cully, *Education for Spiritual Growth*, 43.
2. Jean Grasso Fitzpatrick, *Something More* (New York: Viking, 1991), 26.
3. "Many Believe Influence of Religion is Declining," *Emerging Trends* (September 1990), 2.
4. *The Unchurched American—10 Years Later* (Princeton, NJ: Princeton Religion Research Center, 1988), 32, 33.
5. Quoted in Timothy Jones, "More Than Souls with Ears: George Hunter on Evangelism," *Messenger* (April 1986), 26.
6. Wuthnow, *Acts of Compassion*, 154-55.
7. Princeton Religion Research Center, "Mega Churches or Small Groups?" *Emerging Trends* (October 1991), 1.
8. Ibid., 6.
9. Unpublished portion of interview with Timothy Jones, "More than Souls with Ears: George Hunter on Evangelism."
10. *Unchurched American*, 3.
11. Cully, *Education for Spiritual Growth*, 126.
12. Ibid.
13. Wuthnow, *Acts of Compassion*, 159.
14. *Unchurched American*, 32–33.
15. The Rev. David Stokes, in newsletter of All Saints' Episcopal Church, Princeton, New Jersey.
16. Princeton Religion Research Center, "God Not Just an Abstract Concept to Teens," *Emerging Trends* (October 1991), 2.
17. *Faith Development and Your Ministry* (Princeton, NJ: Princeton Religion Research Center, 1985), 60.
18. William O'Malley, "Toward an Adult Spirituality," *America* (November 18, 1989), 341.

19. "The Boomers Are Back!" *Newsweek* (December 17, 1990), 51.
20. Ibid.
21. *Unchurched American*, 33.
22. Donald Joy, quoted in a forum article, "Building Faith," *Christianity Today* (June 13, 1986), 4–I.
23. Cully, *Education for Spiritual Growth*, 35.
24. Arthur Paul Boers, "Recovering our Testimonies," *Christian Living* (March 1991), 8–9.
25. Robert L. Wilken, "The Lives of the Saints and the Pursuit of Virtue," *First Things* (December 1990), 50.

86154